MENSA GUIDE TO
BLACKJACK

**Official Mensa
Puzzle Book**

Joshua Hornik

STERLING PUBLISHING CO., INC.

NEW YORK

Dedication

To Lauri, for her support,
and to "Nick" who taught me
everything I know.

Mensa and the distinctive table logo are trademarks of
American Mensa, Ltd. (in the U.S.),
British Mensa, Ltd. (in the U.K.),
Australian Mensa, Inc. (in Australia),
and Mensa International Limited (in other countries)
and are used by permission.

Library of Congress Cataloging-in-Publication Data

Hornik, Joshua.
Mensa guide to blackjack / Joshua Hornik.
p. cm. Includes index.
ISBN 1-4027-0979-X
1. Blackjack. I. Mensa. II. Title.
GV1295.H67 2005
795.4'23--dc22
2005001143

2 4 6 8 10 9 7 5 3 1

Published by Sterling Publishing Co., Inc.
387 Park Avenue South, New York, NY 10016
© 2005 by Joshua Hornik
Distributed in Canada by Sterling Publishing
c/o Canadian Manda Group, 165 Dufferin Street
Toronto, Ontario, Canada M6K 3H6
Distributed in Great Britain by Chrysalis Books Group PLC
The Chrysalis Building, Bramley Road, London W10 6SP, England
Distributed in Australia by Capricorn Link (Australia) Pty. Ltd.
P.O. Box 704, Windsor, NSW 2756, Australia

Manufactured in the United States of America
All rights reserved

Sterling ISBN: 1-4027-0979-X

For more information about custom editions, special sales, premium and
corporate purchases, please contact Sterling Special Sales
Department at 800-805-5489 or specialsales@sterlingpub.com

CONTENTS

INTRODUCTION

There is a well-known saying among poker players: "When you sit down to play cards, look around the table. If you cannot spot the sucker, then it's probably you."

It's a phrase based in fact. An unskilled poker player will be simply cleaned out by a table full of more experienced and better players. It's possible that a lucky player could win a few hands, maybe even win a big pot with a great hand, and defeat a better poker player. But given enough time and enough of a bankroll, a truly talented poker player will always beat an unskilled player.

CAN YOU SPOT THE SUCKERS?

Walk into any casino at any time of the day or night and chances are there will be plenty of folks laying down hard-earned money, hoping against hope that they can get lucky and beat the casino. Take a good look in any direction and you'll see people gambling—at video machines, at felt tables, watching sports on big-screen TVs, tossing dice, holding cards, spinning wheels, and pulling handles (or just pushing buttons on today's virtual slot machines). Well, have you spotted the suckers in the casino yet?

How about the slot machine players? They are the bread and butter of casino cash flows, pouring nickel after nickel, quarter after quarter, even dollar after dollar into the machines. Okay, every once in a while someone wins a jackpot and goes home happy. But slot machines aren't games of chance any more. These days, they are all computers that are programmed to take 5 to 10 percent of the player's money. Computers don't make mistakes. They don't get confused, or drunk, or forget the rules. If a computer is programmed to take 10 percent of your money, it will do just that. Where does that leave all those slot machine players? It makes them 10 percent poorer.

Okay, now let's take roulette players. Again, they're usually hanging in there, looking for that big score when their numbers come up. Let's do the math. There are 36 numbers plus 0 and 00 on an American roulette wheel. (European roulette wheels generously only contain one zero.) So you have a 1 in 38 chance of hitting your number. But what does that bet pay? 35 to 1. Betting this and all other roulette bets will lose a player, in time, over 5 percent of his stake. Yet another sucker bet.

Maybe you've heard that craps is one of the best games a discerning gambler can play. Let's take a look at those craps players. They're the ones clapping, yelling, and seeming to be having the best time, so they must be winning, right? Let's assume the player understands and uses perfect craps strategy to maximize the odds. (And let's be honest, how many people in the crowd at the craps table do you think really do?) By playing correctly and taking advantage of the odds, a skilled craps player can reduce the casino's edge to below 1 percent. Not bad, but it still means the player will be losing money. And a person who plays a game knowing that he is expected to lose his money might just be the definition of a sucker.

In fact, when you look around a casino at all the gamblers, you will find that everyone you look at is a sucker. That's why casinos make so much money and keep getting bigger and bigger. Like P.T. Barnum said, "There is a sucker born every minute." And in a world of 24-hour casinos, that's a lot of minutes.

HOW <u>NOT</u> TO BE A SUCKER

Now look over at the blackjack table. There are probably quite a few suckers there, too. But look closely and you may find someone very rare: a winner. This is because blackjack is a casino game that can be beaten. By counting cards, a blackjack player moves the edge from the casino's favor over to the player's side. Counting cards is not illegal. It does not break any blackjack rules. It simply means using the knowledge of the cards and your own intelligence to make bets more wisely and gain the edge over the casino.

If a card counter at the blackjack table is very good, you will not know that he is counting cards. (After all, if the casino knew it was happening, they'd see that it stopped. They only want suckers at their tables.) But the card counter is playing according to solid blackjack strategy, and betting according to mathematics and probability based on the cards that have already been played (and, consequently, those that are left to be played). The card counter's advantage is small, but he has an overall edge, which means, in time, he *will* win money.

WHAT THIS BOOK WILL TEACH YOU

By buying this book, you have taken a step toward becoming a winner. In this book, I will present a very simple method for winning at blackjack, by using basic blackjack strategy and counting cards. I will first discuss the rules of blackjack and the strategies every blackjack player should use to increase his/her chances of winning. Next, I will teach you how to count cards, and, more important, how to use that information to bet high when you win and low when you lose. If you've got a lot of money and a group of like-minded friends, you might want to form a team to increase your chances of winning. I'll show you how to do that, too.

This book is meant to be a practical guide to winning at blackjack. It can be used by the novice playing blackjack for the first time, as well as the advanced player looking to improve his odds of winning. I will not make your head spin with number theory and probabilities down to the thousandth of a percent, but I will hopefully give you just enough of the math behind the play that you will have faith that this method really works. I will provide many examples, as well as tips, on how to practice the skills I teach in the book. For the newcomer to casinos, I'll provide some useful information on what to expect and how to behave like a pro at a blackjack table.

Gambling is considered by most to be a form of entertainment, not an investment or a moneymaking scheme. It's fun, and nothing could be more fun than beating the casino at its own game and making a little money at the same time. That is what this book will teach you to do. I won't say "good luck"—with this book, you don't need luck any more—but "have fun!"

THE RULES OF BLACKJACK

In blackjack, or 21, there is only one bet per hand. Only one person plays his hand at a time. And the hands are played based on a few very basic rules. Compare this to a game like craps, where ten people are placing bets on dozens of choices all over the board, simultaneously, with crazy odds for each bet, and it is easy to see why someone might think blackjack a simple game. A player could easily sit down at a blackjack table, watch a few hands, and feel pretty confident he had learned the rules. However, although the rules of blackjack are deceptively simple, a thorough knowledge of the rules is imperative to becoming a winning player.

Imagine a total stranger to baseball being invited to play in a game. After watching a few players come up to bat, this new player might feel like he understood the game. He would probably know well enough that he had to stand at home plate and hit the pitch and run to first base. However, without knowing all the rules, the new player might not know he can stretch a good hit to a double or a triple, steal second or third base, or run when his teammate hits the ball. In other words, he knew the basic rules but not the details required to be a very good baseball player.

Plays like splitting aces or doubling with an eleven are the blackjack equivalent of stretching hits into doubles and triples, or stealing bases. Knowing when to surrender a poor hand to save half your bet is the equivalent of knowing when to place a sacrifice bunt to move a base runner along. Without fully understanding the rules of blackjack, you can never be a complete player, and certainly not a winner.

For example, let's explore this scenario, which takes place at the blackjack table:

PLAYER: "Hmm . . . Two fives . . . Can I double with this?"
DEALER: "You could double . . . or you could split them, if you want."
PLAYER: "Oh, I can split them? Maybe I'll do that . . ."

Here is a conversation between a dealer and a player who does not know the rules of blackjack. The player should know that, with two fives, he can double or split or simply hit or stand. The correct play (as will be described in Chapter 3) is to double. But because this player didn't know the rules, he ended up drawn into splitting his fives.

A knowledgeable and friendly dealer may have told the player not only the rules but also the best play. But the dealer can't be expected to help the player—some dealers know how to deal but not how best to play; some may just not feel like helping a novice player—and not knowing the rules puts the player at the dealer's mercy.

Learn the rules and don't rely on the dealer, or other players at the table.

HOW TO WIN AT BLACKJACK

How do you win at blackjack? It's very simple. Just get more points than the dealer, without going over 21. That is the most important rule of blackjack. It is you versus the dealer; the other players at the table don't matter. If you have 18 and the dealer has 17, you win. If you have 17 and the dealer has 18, you lose. If you draw to 22, you lose, and then it doesn't matter what the dealer has.

If the dealer goes over 21, and you did not, then you win. So, even if you stop with a 2♣ and 3♥, for a total of five (which, by the way, is not suggested), you will still win if the dealer ends up with 22. Note that the dealer always plays *after* all of the players have played their hands completely.

A winning hand in blackjack pays even odds, 1-to-1. That means if you bet $10, you win $10. If you bet $100, you win $100. This makes it easy to calculate your winnings (and check up on dealers, who have been known to make mistakes in payouts). It also makes it easy to fall for schemes like doubling your bet after you lose in order to make back what you just lost. (This doesn't work. What happens when you lose five or six in a row? Believe me, that's possible.)

The only exception to the 1-to-1 payouts is blackjack (see below), which pays 3-to-2 odds, or 1½ times your bet. If you bet $10 and you get blackjack, you win $15. If you bet $100, you win $150. That is, of course, unless the dealer also happens to get blackjack. In this case, you tie.

When you and the dealer both finish with the same point total (or you both get blackjacks), it is a tie, or push. You don't win anything or lose anything. You just get your bet back. In a game where you lose more hands than you win, you will quickly start to feel like you've won when you manage a push.

HOW TO COUNT TO 21

In order to determine your final point value (and the dealer's), you must know what each card is worth. Twos through tens are, conveniently enough, equal to the face value of the card, or 2 through 10, respectively. Jacks, queens, and kings (in other words, all face cards) are also equal to 10 points. The suit of the card does not matter, only the value.

For example, 2♣ 5♠ K♥ equals 17 (2 + 5 + 10 = 17). 4♥ 4♦ 4♠ 10♥ equals 22, one too many (4 + 4 + 4 + 10 = 22). J♦ Q♠ equals 20 (10 + 10 = 20).

The counting of aces is probably the most confusing rule in blackjack. An ace can count as 1 point, or it can count as 11. In general, you will consider an ace to be worth 11 points, until your total adds up to more than 21, at which point you may think of the ace as only 1 point. Let's take a few examples. A♣ 8♥ equals 19, taking the ace for 11 points (11 + 8 = 19). A♣ 3♥ makes 14 (11 + 3 = 14), but if we then take another card and get a 9♠, rather than 23 (a losing hand), we would have 13. Our hand would be A♣ 3♥ 9♠. Taking the ace now as only 1 point, we have 1 + 3 + 9 = 13. Often, a dealer will say aloud both possible totals for a hand that includes an ace. Therefore, looking at A♥ 5♦, a dealer would say "6 or 16."

A hand that counts an ace as 11 points is called a "soft" hand. In other words, A♦ 6♦ is called a "soft 17." A hand that includes a 1-point ace is called "hard." For example, A♦ 6♦ K♦ is a "hard 17." After adding the 10 points for the king, the ace is now 1 point, and there is no way to

AT THE TABLE

Who can blame a dealer for making jokes and keeping things light and friendly at the table? It makes the game go faster and everyone has more fun—but not when the dealer is having his fun at your expense. Here's a classic joke whereby dealers take advantage of slow counters and novices:

Player's hand: A♠ 2♣. Dealer says "13."

Player takes another card: A♠ 2♣ 3♥. Dealer says "16."

Player takes another card: A♠ 2♣ 3♥ 10♠. Dealer says "26."

Of course, with an ace in the hand, the soft 16 has now become a hard 16 and not a 26. But a beginner will usually be just confused enough by this to think he has actually busted. And the dealer and the fellow players at the table will all have a good laugh at his expense. Be warned: learn to count aces, or prepare to look like a rookie.

change the total of 17, so it is "hard," not "soft." Soft hands are obviously much more versatile and, therefore, more valuable in blackjack.

PRACTICE MAKES PERFECT

Counting your hand's value seems simple, but you should practice enough that it becomes second nature. You will need to see your hand and know instantly how much you have, because when you start to count cards you have to concentrate on that count and not on the value of the cards in your hand. You will also want to be quick enough to count the dealer's cards and know immediately whether you have won or lost. (Dealers do make mistakes, so you need to double-check and make sure to stop a dealer from raking your bet when you have, in fact, won the hand.)

Here's a simple way to practice counting your point totals. Take a deck of cards and hold it face down. One at a time, deal cards off the top of the deck. As you put a card down, count the hand total out loud. When your total goes over 21, start over with a new hand.

Example: 4♥ (Total: 4) 7♦ (Total: 11) 9♥ (Total: 20) 3♣ (Total: 23) Start over.

Don't forget to count aces as you would in the real game.

Example: 3♣ (Total: 3) A♠ (Total: 14; the ace is 11 points) 9♥ (Total: 13; now the ace is 1 point) K♣ (Total: 23) Start over.

Practice this drill, dealing faster and faster, until counting your hand is almost automatic and requires no conscious calculation.

BLACKJACK: THE PLAYER'S BEST FRIEND

When a player gets 21 points on his first two cards, that is, an ace and a face card or ten, he has blackjack. Obviously, this is the best hand possible. The player need not take any more cards and there is no way the dealer can beat this hand. A dealer may also pull an ace and face card or ten, but this worst-case scenario is still just a push, not a loss.

Blackjack pays 3-to-2, a 50 percent bonus over a regular winning hand. For this reason, it is the blackjacks you get in a session that give you your greatest edge.

Example of a blackjack table

(This is also a reason counting cards works. It enables you to know when you have a better chance of getting a blackjack.) A blackjack table is generally a pretty subdued place, certainly in comparison with the boisterous craps table crowds, but when you hear a scream or two from a blackjack table, it's a good bet someone drew a blackjack.

But why, you're probably wondering, is it called "blackjack"? When the game was originally played, under the name Twenty-one, there was no bonus for getting 21 on the first two cards. It was a new innovation to give a bonus to any player who got that 21 on only a black ace and jack. Thus, the name "blackjack." Luckily for us players, the bonus soon became standard for any natural 21, regardless of color.

ORDER OF PLAY

Casino games are nothing if not consistent. In order to insure equal odds for all, the rules do not change and the games are played the same way every time. In blackjack, that means that the game will be played in the same order every time, with the dealer following strict rules and performing some actions over and over exactly

the same, like a well-rehearsed performer.

A round of blackjack starts with all the players placing their bets. There will be a circle or spot (sometimes signified with a themed picture or text) on the table where you should place your bet. (See the illustration on this page.) After all bets are placed, the dealer will deal one card to each player, followed by one card face down to himself.

In casinos, you will find some blackjack games are played using only one or two decks of cards, while others are played with "shoes" of six or eight decks. The rules of the game do not depend on the number of decks. However, in single- and double-deck blackjack games, the player's cards are dealt face down and the player will pick up the cards and look at them. In one- or two-deck games, the dealer will deal the cards from a pack in his hand, while six- and eight-deck games require a plastic box called a "shoe" that holds the cards (because dealers who can hold eight decks of cards in one hand are rather difficult to find). In six- and eight-deck games, the cards are dealt face up and the player is not allowed to touch the cards. After the players and dealer all have their first cards,

AT THE TABLE

When playing blackjack at a casino, you need to know the correct hand signals for hitting and standing. While you can easily just say to a dealer "hit" or "stand," it is not enough to just say it. There are cameras watching every table, both to watch for criminal activity and cheating and to ensure correct play. The videotape from these cameras serves as a backup if a player feels he has been wronged. Therefore, hand signals are required, so that they may be reviewed later from the videotape (which does not include sound).

The signal for "stand" is to wave your hand back and forth across the top of your hand. The signal for "hit" is to hit the table behind your cards. There are many variations on this signal. You may knock the table with a fist, or slap it with an open hand. You may hit it extra hard with a yell when looking for a very lucky draw. Or you may want to just point at or tap the table with one finger. Just be careful which finger you use, or else you might insult your dealer.

If you are playing at a one- or two-deck blackjack table, you will be holding your cards. Rather than pointing at the table, you signal that you want a hit by scraping the cards you are holding towards yourself on the table (signifying "send another card my way, chief"). The signal for "stand" is to place your cards face down on the table, under your bet, to signify that you are done with the hand.

the dealer deals a second card to each player, then another card for himself, turning only one of his cards face up.

Play then starts with the first player to the dealer's left. (The first seat to the dealer's left is called "first base" because it is the first to play. The first seat to the dealer's right, or the last around the table to his left, is called "third base.") This player will take cards as desired until he busts or is satisfied with his hand. Play then moves to the player to that player's left. Play moves in this way clockwise across the table, until all players have completed their hands.

When all players have played their hands, the dealer will turn over his "hole card," the one card he had already dealt face down to himself. The dealer will then play his hand, according to strict and unchanging rules (see below), to comple-tion. At this point, the dealer will go clockwise around the table, paying out winning hands or taking losing bets, as necessary.

TO HIT OR TO STAND

Although in certain cases the player has other options, the player always has the choice of hitting (taking another card) or standing (ending his hand as it is).

If a player chooses to stand, his hand is complete at the current point value. Play moves to the player to his left, or the dealer if he was the last player at the table. *Example:* Q♥ 9♦. The player has 19, so he stands, and is done. If the dealer ends up with a 17, 18, or busts, the player wins. A 19 is a push, while the dealer can beat the player only with 20 or 21.

If a player chooses to hit, the dealer will deal one card, face up, on top of his hand.

AT THE TABLE

There is no special signal for doubling, but there is a rule for how to add to your bet. You will already have a chip (or stack of chips, if you're a high roller) in the betting circle. To signify that you want to double, you should place an equal amount (the same chip or stack of chips) next to the original bet in the circle. This is usually enough for the dealer to understand you want to double, and to give you your one card. You may put the extra bet out as soon as you've received your cards, or you may wait until your turn at the table. Unfortunately, you can't wait until after you see the 10 that gives you 21 to double your bet.

In the case when your two cards are a pair (like 5♥ 5♦ or 4♠ 4♣) and you want to double, you will have to say "double" or "one card" to the dealer, so that he doesn't think you want to split your hand. Of course, this should only happen when you have a pair of fives, for a 10. If you are thinking of doubling any other pair, then you had better read Chapter 3 on basic strategy!

Why put the chips next to the original bet? Why not just throw them on top of your original bet and make one neat little pile? This rule is to prevent cheating. It would be very easy for someone to add more than the original bet and put it in one big pile. The dealer can't remember how much each person bet originally, so he would have no way of knowing what part of the pile was there before and what was new. This way, you could "triple down" or even "quadruple down." With two stacks side-by-side, it's very easy for the dealer to check and make sure they're the same height.

When the dealer deals the next card onto your hand, he will turn the card to the side to signify that it is the last card you get and your hand is complete. Sometimes, a dealer will make the game a little more exciting by turning the card face down. Because you cannot take any more cards, it really doesn't matter what the card is until the dealer completes his hand. Then, the dealer will turn over the card on your hand and you find out whether you won or not. Of course, if you bet a lot on that double, you may not quite appreciate the excitement of not knowing whether you got the card you wanted.

The value of that card will be added to the hand value, and the play will continue as before. Again, the player will be asked to choose to hit or to stand. *Example:* 5♣ 4♣. The player has only 9, so he takes a hit. The dealer deals him a J♥. He now has 19, so he stands.

DOUBLING DOWN

How many times have you made a bet, then wished you had bet more after you saw that you had good cards? Blackjack is a game that actually lets you add to your bet after you've seen your cards. This is called "doubling down."

In most casinos, you are allowed to "double down" on your first two cards. When you double down, you double the bet you made on the hand and take exactly one more card. You will make use of this rule when you have the start of a good hand (such as a 10 or 11). You are at a disadvantage because you are only allowed one more card, even if it turns out to be very bad (like a 2 or 3). However, as long as you only double when you have a good chance of winning, you will earn a lot of extra money with this rule.

Example: You have bet $10 and you are dealt 8♥ 3♣. The dealer shows a 6♠. This is a perfect hand for doubling. You place another $10 down, making your bet now equal $20. You get one card: a K♠. You now have 8♥ 3♣ K♠, for 21, an unbeatable hand, and your bet is now $20, not just $10.

Doubling is generally done by, as you would expect, doubling your bet, or adding an amount equal to what you had originally bet. However, it is within the rules to "double for less," or add an amount lower than your original bet. This is not recommended. If the cards are good for doubling, you should take full advantage of the rule and add the maximum allowed to your bet. If you are doubling for less because you don't have enough to exactly double your bet, it means you were betting too high for your bankroll. You should always have enough money to cover splits and doubles.

SPLITTING

When your first two cards are a pair (like 5♥ 5♦ or 4♠ 4♣), you can "split" your hand into two separate hands with one card each. The dealer will then deal you new cards in addition to your original cards, and each hand will be played individually. Splitting will also double the amount you have bet in that round, but while doubling down puts all your money on one hand, splitting gives you two chances to win the hand. Which means, you could win both hands and win double your original bet, or lose both hands and lose double your original bet. But you could also win one hand and lose the other, the equivalent of a push.

To split your hand, just like doubling, you will add an amount equal to your original bet. You cannot "split for less." You must always bet the same amount on both post-split hands. After you have added your second bet, the dealer will split your two cards into two hands side by side. Then, the dealer will deal one card onto the first hand. Before you get the second card for your other split hand, you will play your first hand. This hand will be played exactly like any other blackjack hand. After your first hand is complete (i.e., you either busted or stood with what you have), the dealer will move on to the next hand. He will deal one card onto the second hand, and that hand will proceed as any other hand.

Example: You have bet $10 and you are dealt 4♥ 4♥. The dealer shows a 6♥. This is a good hand for splitting. You place another $10 next to your original bet. The dealer splits your two fours. He then deals another card onto your first hand. You now have 4♥ 8♥. It's only 12, but you stand. (Trust me—against a six, you don't need to hit that.) The dealer now moves to your second hand, made from the 4♥ you had in your original pair. He deals a second card to the hand. You now have 4♥ 3♥. You take a hit. Another 4, 4♥. You now have 4♥ 3♥ 4♥, for 11. Too late to double, so you take another hit and get a 10♥, for a 21. Great! Now you know at least you won't lose $20 on the hand.

Splitting hands can be very lucrative. This is because you play most post-split hands exactly the same as you would any other hand, which means that you can also double and split these hands. So, you may start with a $10 bet, then split it to two

AT THE TABLE

Here's another table rule from those paranoid casinos: Never touch the cards. At least in six- and eight-deck blackjack games, only the dealer is allowed to touch the cards. So, when you want to split your two cards into two hands, though it is tempting to grab one of the cards and move it over, you should let the dealer move the cards. This is another rule to thwart cheating, such as marking cards or switching cards when the dealer isn't looking.

To signify that you want to split, just put the new bet next to the original bet. While you put a "double" bet right next to your original bet, you may want to place your additional "split" bet a little distance from the original bet. (If you don't, the dealer usually will move it anyway, so that the bets for each hand do not get confused.) You will probably also have to say "split" in cases when the dealer can't be sure that's what you want to do.

Splitting aces is a special case. Because the ace is such a good card to play with, the casinos make it a little tougher on you when you split aces. You will only be allowed one additional card on an ace when you split. As in a double, the dealer will place the cards sideways on your aces, to signify that your hands are complete. You are hoping that you will get a ten or face card with your ace, to make 21. Note that this will be a 21, but not a blackjack. You can only get blackjack (and get paid 3-to-2) on your original two cards.

Example: You bet $10 and are dealt A♥ A♠. You add another $10 and split your aces. The dealer deals one card to each hand. (You get no choice to hit or stand. You must always stand.) You get a J♠ on the first. Yahtzee! You get a 3♣ on the second. D'oh! Oh well, at least you probably won't do worse than a push (win one, lose one), and maybe the dealer will bust.

The casinos limit the number of times you can re-split a hand. In other words, if you had 4♥ 4♦ and you split, and are dealt a 4♣, and split again, and are dealt a 4♠, you could split a fourth time. But in most casinos, you will be stopped at four hands. In some casinos, you will be stopped at only two or three hands. Obviously, the more times you are allowed to re-split, the better for you, because you only split when the odds favor your hand. In addition, some casinos will allow you to re-split aces (if you split aces, and get another ace for your one card), while some will force you to play the post-split aces as 12 (A♥ A♣ is 11 + 1 = 12). Again, it is much better for you if the casino lets you re-split aces, because 12 is such a bad hand, but split aces have the potential of being two very good hands.

You will also find some casinos that do not allow you to double down on a hand after you have split your original hand. This, too, is just a way for casinos to add to their edge over the players. It is certainly better to be able to double when you get a good hand, whether it was your original hand or a post-split hand. Because the number of times that you will come across this situation is small, however, this rule doesn't take too much away from the player. (Which is probably also the reason most casinos don't bother with this rule. Most casinos will allow doubling down after splitting.)

$10 bets, then double both of them, making two $20 bets, for a total of $40 rather than your original $10 bet.

Example: You have bet $10 and are dealt 4♥ 4♠. You split the fours into two $10 bets. For your first hand, the dealer deals you a 6♦. You now have 4♥ 6♦, for 10, so you double. Your bet on this hand is now $20, and you get a 9♣, for a 19. On your second hand, the dealer deals you another 4♥. You now have 4♥ 4♥ for your second hand, so you split this hand, too. You now have one bet of $20 and two bets of $10. On your second hand, you get a 3♣ and then a K♠, for a 17 (4♥ 3♣ K♠). On your third hand, you get a 7♦, for 11 (4♥ 7♦). You double again. You now have one bet of $20, one bet of $10, and another bet of $20. You get a 5♦, for a measly 16 (4♥ 7♦ 5♦). Remember, you only get one card when you double. Luckily, the dealer busts and you win all your hands for total winnings of $50 on an original bet of $10!

SURRENDERING

Just like those times when you get such good cards you wish you had bet more money, there are also going to be times when you get such bad cards you wish you hadn't bet at all. If only you could pull your bet back and pretend like that hand had never happened. In blackjack, you can't quite do that, but the "surrender" rule does allow you to take half of your bet back.

Surrendering is very simple. If, after your first two cards are dealt, you feel that your chances of winning the hand are extremely poor, you can surrender half of your bet. When it comes to your turn to act on your hand, rather than hitting or standing, you just say "surrender" to the dealer. (The little-known hand signal for

surrendering is to pass your index finger across the table behind your cards, but it is never used in casinos today.) The dealer will count your bet and take half, leaving the other half for you to take back. The dealer will rake your cards and you will not complete your hand. (You don't want to know, anyway. Just assume you would have lost, and you will be happy to only lose half of your bet.)

Example: You have bet $10 and are dealt 9♥ 7♣. The dealer is showing a K♥. You feel pretty bad about your chances with a 16 against a 10 for the dealer, so you decide to surrender. You say "surrender" when the dealer comes to you. The dealer takes your cards and takes $5 from your original $10 bet, leaving you with $5. It is a $5 loss, but the next card out is a Q♦, which would have busted you, so you actually saved $5 by surrendering.

The most common form of surrender is more specifically called "late surrender," because you can only take advantage of the rule after the dealer has checked to see if he has a blackjack. When the dealer has blackjack, you will lose your entire bet before you get the option of surrendering. Although you will be hard pressed to find any casinos providing it, there is also a rule called "early surrender." With early surrender, you can surrender half your bet before the dealer checks his hand. Obviously, early surrender is a much more advantageous rule for the player, because it allows a player to surrender a poor hand when the dealer is showing an ace and protect himself from a dealer blackjack, as well as a bad hand. That is why you probably won't find any casinos offering it these days.

While surrendering seems like a great deal for the casinos (after all, they get half your original bet, without any chance of you winning), it is actually a very favorable rule for the player. In fact, of the many optional house rules you will find in various casinos, surrendering adds the biggest edge to the player, worth a full 0.5 percent. You will find that only about half of all casinos offer the surrender rule, so be aware of the house rules before you play.

INSURANCE

When the dealer deals himself an ace, you will feel a pain in the pit of your stomach. Odds are better that the dealer has blackjack (i.e., a ten or face card hidden underneath that ace) than any other hand. And if the dealer gets blackjack, you lose before you even get a chance to play your hand in most casinos. Your only hope is to get a blackjack yourself, and then it's still only a push.

For the truly risk-averse, casinos invented the "insurance" rule. When the dealer shows an ace, he opens the table to making an insurance bet. It is called "insurance" because it ensures that, if the dealer has blackjack, you will not lose your money. To take this bet, you will put an amount equal to half your original bet into the area on the table marked insurance. After every player who wants to has bet on insurance, the hands will be played as usual. If the dealer turns out to have blackjack, the insurance bet will be paid, but the original hand bet will be taken (because all hands but blackjack are losers to a dealer's blackjack). The final result for the player who bet on insurance is a push. If the dealer turns out not to have blackjack, the insurance bet is lost.

Example: You have bet $10 and are dealt 5♥ 6♦ (a good hand), but the dealer turns over an A♠. The dealer asks if anyone wants insurance. You decide to take insurance, so you place $5 on the insurance spot on the table. The dealer checks and, sure enough, has a J♠ under the A♠, for blackjack. Your 5♥ 6♦ is a loser and you lose your $10. But your insurance bet is a winner and, at 2-to-1 odds, a $5 bet pays $10. You break even.

Insurance really is a bet that the dealer has blackjack, and it pays 2-to-1. Therefore, by betting half the original bet, if the dealer does turn out to have blackjack, you will win two times your insurance bet, or an amount equal to your original bet. However, at the same time, you lose that original bet, which means you come out exactly even.

If you, the player, have blackjack and the dealer turns over an ace, you may be asked if you want "even money." That is the same as the dealer asking if you want insurance. That is because if you have blackjack and you bet insurance, whether the dealer has blackjack or not you will win 1-to-1 odds on your bet, or even money. To understand, let's look at an example.

Example: You have bet $10 and are dealt A♠ J♥. Blackjack! But the dealer has an A♣ showing. You decide to take insurance, so you bet $5, half your original bet, in the insurance spot. If the dealer turns over his hole card and has blackjack, you win $10 for your insurance bet, but because your blackjack is a push and not a loss, you also get to keep your original bet. Therefore, you come out ahead $10, or the same amount as your original bet. If, instead, the dealer didn't have blackjack, you would lose your insurance bet of $5. However, your blackjack would be worth 3-to-2, or $15. Again, you win $10 ($15 win minus $5 loss).

Even money sounds very enticing. You always win! But don't forget that if you hadn't taken insurance and the dealer didn't have blackjack, you would have won $15, not just $10. That's a 50 percent difference, just for the safety of knowing you'll always win.

THE DEALER'S RULES

After all of the players have completed their turns, it is the dealer's turn to play his hand. The dealer has a set of very simple rules to follow in playing his hand. These rules never change, so the players always know what to expect from the dealer. This is very important for forming a strategy for how to play your hands. (See Chapter 3 on basic blackjack strategy.)

The rules for the dealer are as follows:

1. The dealer always hits a hand of 16 or lower.
2. The dealer always stands with a 17 or higher.
3. The dealer never splits pairs.
4. For the dealer, the ace is also either 11 points or 1 point, but the dealer will use it as a 1 *only* when an 11 would cause the dealer to bust.

The dealer will first turn over his hole card. If the two cards (the up card and the hole card) add up to a total of 17 or higher, the dealer stops there. If the two cards add up to 16 or lower, the dealer will take cards until the hand is 17 or higher, or the dealer has busted.

In some casinos, the dealer will also hit a soft 17 (an ace plus 6) and only stand on hard 17s. This is a house rule that you must watch out for.

The rules for the dealer will generally be printed on the blackjack table itself. On the felt, you will see printed "Dealer stands on all 17s" or, in the case of this house rule, "Dealer hits soft 17s." Make sure you know what rules the dealer will be following before you sit down. In fact, it is better for the casino when the dealer hits soft 17s, so it is in your best interest to find a blackjack table where the dealer will stand on all 17s. Sometimes you will find a casino that has some tables with one rule and some tables with the other rule, so look around when you get to the casino. Sometimes, you are better off finding a different casino completely.

NOW PRACTICE PLAYING

Now you know all the rules of blackjack and should be able to play at a casino without looking like a complete amateur. It is a good idea to practice playing, so that you become familiar with all of the rules. You will not always need to use the double, split, or surrender rules, so you will need to get quite a few hands under your belt to get used to those rules. The best way to be sure you understand all the rules is to play a lot of hands.

But going out to the casino with a pocketful of cash and just your knowledge of the rules would be a very good way to lose that money. Just because you know how to *play* blackjack doesn't mean you know how to *win*. For that, you'll need the rest of this book.

There are other ways to practice blackjack without going to a casino and putting your money at risk. There is blackjack software you can download or buy that will act exactly the same as a casino. (You can even set different house rules, such as re-splitting and allowing surrender.) You can also find a lot of free blackjack games on the Internet. Be careful that you are playing a free game, though, because there are also a lot of blackjack games online on which you'll be playing for real money.

With blackjack software or a free online game, you can play in the privacy of your own home, on your computer, without losing any money. You can play as many hands as you want, until you feel perfectly comfortable splitting, re-splitting, doubling down, surrendering, or just hitting to get that five that turns your 16 into 21.

REVIEW QUESTIONS

At the end of most chapters, I will include a few review questions. Use these to test your knowledge of the contents of the chapter, and for review after taking some time away from playing blackjack. The questions are not difficult. They are meant only to represent the basic information discussed in the chapter. The answers are found on pages 119 to 123.

First, some blackjack hand counting practice. For the first three questions, look at the cards listed and add up the value of the hands they represent.

1. 3♥ 5♣ 6♦ 2♣ 4♠
2. A♦ 8♥
3. A♠ 3♠ 8♣ 5♦

For the next four questions, look at the cards that make up the player's hand and dealer's up card. What are the possible plays the player can make, by standard blackjack rules?

4. Player: 3♥ 8♥   Dealer: 6♣
5. Player: 5♠ 5♣   Dealer: J♥
6. Player: A♦ 10♣   Dealer: 2♠
7. Player: 8♦ 8♦   Dealer: A♠

8. A player bets $100 and gets a J♥ A♣. The dealer busts. How much does the player win?

9. A player bets $100 and gets a 7♥ 7♦. The player splits and gets a 4♣ on the 7♥. He doubles, and gets a Q♠. On his 7♦, he gets a 10♦ and stands. The dealer ends up with 6♦ J♣ 3♥. How much does the player win or lose?

10. A player bets $100 and gets A♠ K♠. The dealer is showing A♥. The player takes insurance. The dealer has a 7♣ to go with his A♥. How much does the player win or lose?

ALTERNATIVE BLACKJACK GAMES

When you go to a casino, you will find many tables used for playing blackjack. Besides slot machines, blackjack is the most popular game at any casino. You will generally be able to find entire pits (several tables forming a circle or oval around an area where casino staff work) devoted entirely to the game of blackjack. Look for the "blackjack" signs hanging down from the ceiling above the tables. You will generally find that all of the tables are playing standard blackjack rules, as described in Chapter 1.

However, you may also find some tables providing unique and different rules, and you may even find tables with a completely different version of the game of blackjack. There are several reasons why casinos experiment with different rules on their games. The first reason is marketing. Casinos have the edge in all games, so the more players a casino can bring in to play at its tables and machines, the more money it will win. Casinos try tweaking the rules to their games to make them more attractive to players. That's why many of the rule changes involve bonuses such as extra winnings for five-card hands or three 7s of the same suit. New rules like these can make the game more interesting and certainly more exciting when they pay off. In addition, casinos try out entirely new games to entice new gamblers. Witness the addition in recent years of games like Pai Gow Poker, Carribean Stud Poker, and Casino War.

Before you get too excited about new rules that will pay bonuses on top of all the winnings you will regularly make playing blackjack, let me tell you the second reason casinos change the rules: to increase their edge. The fact is that, although rule changes may make games seem like they pay more, rules that increase odds are almost always combined with other rule changes that reduce the player's odds of winning. As you will see, the math behind blackjack and most other casino games is confusing and nobody can be expected to calculate odds in his/her head. That plays right into the casinos' hands, allowing them to tweak rules and invent new games that seem more fun and easier to beat but, at the same time, actually have much higher casino edges. For example, look at the huge progressive jackpots found on some slot machines. They seem like a chance at a huge sum, but the statistical truth is that the players of these slots, despite the slim chance of a jackpot, have much lower odds of winning money.

The third reason a casino may try to encourage patrons to play a new game is one that should be particularly interesting to readers of this book. Casinos invent new rules or games to defend against the ways players have found to beat the game. Specifically, casinos have invented new rules and games to try to defeat card counting in blackjack. Go to many casinos today and you will find

---

AT THE TABLE

The new blackjack games in the casino will be near the regular blackjack tables. Because they haven't yet reached the popularity of standard blackjack, you will find that on crowded days in the casino, you may be more likely to find a seat at a Spanish 21 or Double Exposure table than a regular blackjack table. In addition, since these games are designed to lure new gamblers, the limits are usually lower than the blackjack tables. So, if you are looking for a $5 game or an empty table in a crowd, you may find yourself sitting down at one of the alternative near-blackjack games.

Let me warn against playing a game without full knowledge of the rules. These games look very similar (almost identical in the case of Spanish 21) to regular blackjack and it may seem that you can pick up the new rules as you play. Remember that, even if you know all the rules of blackjack cold and understand the perfect way to play every hand, the casino is still expected to win more than half the time. If, instead, you make a few mistakes because you didn't know about a certain rule or special case, the casino's edge grows precipitously. You may think you understand the new rules, while you're giving up a 5 percent or higher edge to the casino.

Make sure you know what game you are playing before you sit down, and that you know all the rules. If you don't know the rules, don't play the game. If it's the only table open and you're desperate to play, play the minimums (and don't expect to win).

---

continuous shuffling machines at card-game tables, including blackjack. While the biggest advantage these machines give the casinos is the ability to fit more hands (which means more money) into an hour or day, it cannot have missed their attention that it is impossible to count cards when they are being constantly shuffled. Spanish 21, which is a new game described below, was invented, many say, as a way to deter card counting by keeping counts artificially low.

This chapter describes some of these new and different blackjack games. They are each different in their own way, and you may even find them to be more fun than standard blackjack. However, they also require unique playing strategies (only the complete basic strategy for playing standard blackjack will be described in this book) and have unique odds. These new games can be beaten, but they are found in fewer casinos and on fewer tables. In terms of your edge, the time it would take to learn each game, and the prevalence of these games, I would suggest that you are better off learning the system in this book for beating a standard blackjack game.

SPANISH 21

Spanish 21 has gained some popularity in casinos in the past few years. You are likely to find one or two Spanish 21 tables in the same pit as the rest of the blackjack tables, or somewhere nearby. A quick look over at a Spanish 21 table and you will likely think you are looking at a regular blackjack table. The game is played almost exactly the same, and the table will look nearly identical, save for the signs on the table and nearby that say "Spanish 21."

Spanish 21 game play is exactly the same as standard blackjack. The players are dealt two cards face up, and the dealer is dealt one card face down and one card face up. In fact, almost all of the rules are the same, but Spanish 21 has some liberal rule adjustments that help the player. In addition, Spanish 21 incorporates bonus payments for special hands, like suited hands that add up to 21, or five- and six-card 21s. The bonuses and liberal rules make the game more fun and exciting for the players, with a chance at a big score, much like a slot machine or poker game.

In Spanish 21, the winner of the hand is decided as in blackjack, with one big exception. The player will win if his hand is higher than the dealer's, or if the dealer goes bust, and the hand is a push if the two hands are tied. However, if the player and dealer both finish with hands of 21, the player wins. This includes blackjack, so, while a player with blackjack only pushes against a dealer blackjack, in Spanish 21, that player will still get paid 3:2 odds. This rule obviously increases the player's chance of winning.

First, let's look at the small changes Spanish 21 makes to standard blackjack rules. One common set of rules you might find at a standard blackjack table includes doubling allowed on any first two cards, splitting of any pair (but only one card on split aces), and late surrender on the first two cards. Spanish 21 allows doubling at any time, on any number of cards. For example, in standard blackjack, you might double when you get 4♦ 6♣ with your first two cards. In Spanish 21, if your first two cards are 4♦ 3♣ and you take a hit and get a 3♠, you might then double and hope for 20.

Some Spanish 21 games even allow re-doubling. With re-doubling, you would be able to double once and, if you still liked your chances, you could double again (effectively multiplying your original bet by four). Because you will only double when you feel you have a good chance of winning, you will win more money by being allowed to double more often, so this is another rule that helps the player.

In Spanish 21, most casinos will allow you to split and re-split hands three times and sometimes even up to four times. In addition, when you split aces, you will not have to stop with only one card on each ace. After you get the new card with your ace, you can hit, double, or stop. You can even re-split your hand if you get another ace. Because you will often double with an ace, this is another rule change that helps the player win.

There is a new rule added to Spanish 21, which is called "double down rescue." The name is quite explanatory: the rule allows you to "rescue" your bet after you double down if you're afraid of losing. After doubling, you receive your card. If you haven't busted, but you don't feel good about your chances of winning the hand, you can surrender your original bet, but then bet your double. This is effectively the same as allowing surrender after a double (because you are giving up half of your new bet, which is equal to twice your original bet). This bet was invented for all those times you get an 11 with your first two cards and double, expecting to hit 21, and get an ace added to your 11, for a big 12.

In addition to all those rule changes that aid the player, there are also several bonuses for hitting 21 in some special way. Hitting 21 with exactly five cards pays 3:2 instead of even odds. Doing it in six cards pays double, while managing 21 in seven cards (or more) pays 3:1 odds. Getting triple your bet is certainly a big score, but think how rare a seven-card 21 really is. Not only must you receive seven cards averaging only 3 in value, but you must also get them in the correct order so that you actually choose to take a hit five times in a row. (Because, if you had gotten a 3♣ 2♣ 5♠ 4♦ 2♠ 2♦, which adds up to 18, would you really take another hit for the chance at getting a 3?)

You can also get a bonus in Spanish 21 for hitting 21 with only three cards, as long as they are the right three cards. Bonuses are awarded for a hand of 6, 7, and 8, or for a hand of three 7s. If the three cards are different suits (for example, 6♣ 7♥ 8♦ or 7♠ 7♦ 7♠), the player gets paid 3:2 odds. If, however, the cards are all the same suit (say, 6♥ 7♥ 8♥ or 7♦ 7♦ 7♦), the player gets paid 2:1 odds. Finally, if the same three cards are all the same suit and that suit is spades, the player gets paid three times his bet.

You have now learned all of the rule changes involved in Spanish 21. You may have noticed that, although in some cases the advantage is slim, all of these rules help the player and not the casino. You are probably thinking that it must be impossible to lose at Spanish 21. Now, here is the catch. (This is a casino. Of course there is a catch.) Remember a Spanish 21 deck contains only 48 cards, instead of the standard 52. Those 48 cards consist of a standard deck with all of the 10s removed. That leaves four jacks, queens, and kings, all of which have a value in blackjack of 10, but the removal of the 10s makes up for all of the benefit provided by the liberal rules in Spanish 21. The casino has gained back the edge. Not only does the removal of the 10s from the deck increase the

casino's edge in any blackjack game, it also makes Spanish 21 a very bad game for a card counter. (For more on why that is, see Chapter 5.)

Do the Math Part I

All of these bonuses described sound great and certainly make the third card an exciting event when you're hitting on 7♠ 7♠, but do they really provide that much value to the player? What are the actual odds of getting a hand of 7♠ 7♠ 7♠? Let's take a full shoe and calculate the actual chance of getting that hand. Obviously, after some cards have been dealt, the odds of getting three 7♠s will either go up (if no 7♠s have been dealt yet) or down (if one or more 7♠s have been dealt and taken out of play).

Most Spanish 21 games use six decks, though you will also find some games using an eight-deck shoe. Each deck contains 48 cards (see below for the reason there are 48, and not 52 cards per deck). Therefore, there are 48 × 6 = 288 different cards in the shoe. That means there are 288 possibilities for the first card, 287 possibilities for the second card (288 minus the 1 for the card you've already been dealt), and 286 possibilities for the third card. Multiply those possibilities, then divide by six (because there are six different ways the same combination of cards can be ordered), and you find that there are 3,939,936 different three-card hands possible in the six-deck shoe.

Of those almost 4 million combinations, how many are made up of three 7♠s? There are six of those cards in the shoe (one in each deck). Therefore, there are 20 (6 × 5 × 4 ÷ 6) possible combinations of 7♠ 7♠ 7♠ hands. That means out of 3,939,936 different three-card hands in a six-deck Spanish 21 shoe, only 20 of those hands are the 7♠ 7♠ 7♠ that pays 3:1. The odds of making that hand are 196,997:1 (a little worse than 3:1, I'd say). As the shoe is played, the odds will get better, since there are fewer possible combinations, but you will also see some of the 7♠s get dealt and discarded. As soon as one of those 7♠s is dealt, the odds go down immensely. There are only five remaining 7♠s, and that means only 10 remaining combinations of three-card 3:1 bonus hands. If we assume one deck is gone, including one 7♠, the new odds of getting a 7♠ 7♠ 7♠ go to 227,528:1.

Do the Math Part 2

Removing the 10s from the decks gives the casino a big advantage, enough to counter all of the player-positive rules in Spanish 21. But why does it help the casino so much? You will find out in later chapters how the 10-value cards help the player who follows basic blackjack strategy, and how an increase in the concentration of those cards in the shoe can mean a better chance of winning. But for now, let's look at just one aspect of the Spanish 21 deck.

The best hand in blackjack is the name of the game itself: blackjack. To make a blackjack, a player needs an ace and a 10-value card. Therefore, removing all the 10s from the decks reduces the player's chance of getting blackjack. Let's look at the odds. In a six-deck shoe of standard 52-card decks, there are 48,516 possible two-card combinations. Of those, 2,304 are blackjacks. There is an approximately 1-in-21 chance of getting a blackjack in a standard six-deck shoe. Remove the 10s from the decks and the numbers change. Now, there are only 41,328 possible two-

card combinations, but only 1,728 of those are blackjacks. Now, your chances of getting a blackjack (and getting paid 3:2) are almost 1-in-24, much worse than with the standard deck. That is just one way that the Spanish 21 deck hurts the player's chances of winning.

Although the deck hurts the player's chances, the rules help the player, and the two even out to make Spanish 21 a game whose casino advantage is not much different from standard blackjack. If you are looking for a change you may want to try Spanish 21, but remember that you will have to play differently because of the different rules. In later chapters, I will discuss some changes to playing strategy for this game.

DOUBLE EXPOSURE BLACKJACK

Double Exposure Blackjack is another new innovation on the game of blackjack. It is perhaps less popular today than Spanish 21, but you are still very likely to find a table or two in bigger casinos. This game is the casino's response to every player who has ever thought "if only I knew what the dealer's hole card is."

The game is called Double Exposure, because both of the dealer's first two cards are exposed to the players. Both of the dealer's cards are dealt face up, revealing the dealer's starting two-card hand to the player before he/she plays his/her hand. Imagine knowing for sure whether there was a 10 under that dealer's 6 or finding out that the frightening queen the dealer is showing is actually sitting on top of a much less scary 6. In both cases, you would know that your chances of winning are very high, since the dealer has 16 and will very likely bust when it comes to his turn, and you could take action accordingly.

Of course, your chances of winning must go up when you know more about the dealer's hand. You will be able to keep hitting your hand until you know you have a winning hand. (Or until you bust, but at least it's better than standing with a 17 when the dealer already has 18.) Alternatively, you could stand with 16 against a dealer with a 9♥ and a 7♠ and expect the dealer to bust. If you had only seen one of those cards, you would have been forced to take a hit to try to beat the dealer's hand. (This will be explained further in the next chapter.) Therefore, the edge goes much more to the player's side when the dealer's hand is played face up.

In the case of Double Exposure, what the casino gives by revealing both dealer cards, the casino takes away by changing the rules. In order to return the edge to the casino, the rules of Double Exposure are weighted heavily in the casino's favor. For starters, blackjack played at Double Exposure tables will use the most advantageous rule set for the casino. At most tables, the dealer will hit on soft 17. Many casinos will restrict your ability to double, allowing you to double only on hands of 9, 10, or 11. Many casinos will not allow doubling after splitting, and some casinos will not allow any re-splitting of hands. Finally, surrender will not be offered. Each of these rules hurts the player to a certain extent.

But this is still not the major difference between Double Exposure and standard blackjack. In Double Exposure, ties go to the dealer. In other words, while in standard blackjack, when you and the dealer both end up with 18, you take back your money (and you're usually pretty happy to do so), in Double Exposure you would lose your money. The only exception is when the player and the dealer both get blackjack. In that case, some Double Exposure games will call it a push, while others will give the win to the player. Don't think the casino too generous when a blackjack tie goes to the player, however. In Double Exposure, blackjacks only pay even money, not 3:2 odds.

Losing all ties is a giant hit to the player's chances of winning money. It affects not only how many hands are won, but even how the player will have to play his/her hand. Think about a player with a K♦ 7♣. In standard blackjack, that hand has some possibilities. If the player stands, the dealer may bust or, if the dealer ends up with 17, at least the player gets a push. In Double Exposure, the possibility of the push is gone because ties go to the dealer. Effectively, in Double Exposure, a hand of 17 is even worse than a hand of 16. The player can never win with 17 unless the dealer busts, but if the player takes a hit, he/she is even more likely to bust than when hitting on 16.

It is fun to play Double Exposure, feeling like you suddenly have the power instead of the dealer, but it is not as easy as it seems like it should be. Yes, when the dealer has a big hand like a K♠ 9♣ or 7♣ A♦, you are able to keep hitting your hand until you beat the dealer or bust trying. But all the other dealer hands, like A♦ 2♣ and 3♦ 5♥, require different strategies and they are not always obvious. Once again, the uninitiated player is likely to make playing mistakes without even knowing it. This is a clear example of a game the casinos invented to lure players who think it looks like an easy way to beat the dealer using common sense.

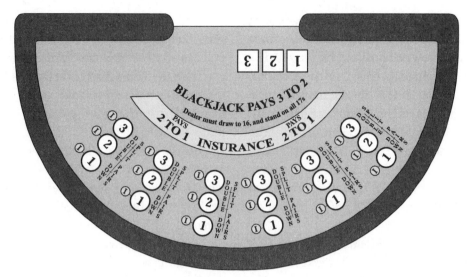

Multiple-action blackjack table

MULTIPLE-ACTION BLACKJACK

Of the variations on blackjack you will find in a casino, Multiple-Action Blackjack is the one that looks the most different from standard blackjack, but it is actually the game that is the most similar. In fact, the rules of Multiple-Action Blackjack are almost identical to regular blackjack, and the odds are indeed the same.

When you look at the Multiple-Action Blackjack table, you will see a lot more spots on the table than normal. There are three rectangles in front of the dealer for his cards. And instead of one circle at each seat for the player to place his bet, there are three circles at each player's seat. The big difference between standard blackjack and Multiple-Action Blackjack is that the latter allows the player to make multiple bets on each of his hands. In fact, a player can place up to three bets on each hand. The player will play the same hand for each of the bets, but the dealer's hands will change for each bet.

Play in Multiple-Action Blackjack starts the same way as regular blackjack: the players place their bets. However, a player may place his bet in all three circles in front of him. After all bets are placed, the dealer deals the cards. As usual, each player will get two cards placed in front of him/her. The dealer will receive one card face up on the first of his three rectangles. The dealer will not deal a hole card. The one up card will be the dealer's first card for three separate hands, so the players will make decisions on their hands based on that one card. Players will play all of their hands to completion, before the dealer plays his hand.

The rules of Multiple-Action Blackjack are the same as regular blackjack, which include the rules for doubling down. If the player wants to double (for example, if he has a 5♥ 6♣ and the dealer is showing a 5♠), he has the choice of doubling all three of his bets or only one of the bets. As in standard blackjack rules, the player also can double down for less than the original bet on one, two, or all three of his bets. (Of course, as in standard blackjack, it is in the player's best interest to take full advantage and bet exactly double on all bets.)

In standard blackjack, a player may not

split for less. Splits can only be made with equal bets on each hand. That rule stands in Multiple-Action Blackjack, as well. If a player has made a bet in all three circles, and receives an 8♣ 8♠, he may split the 8s, but he must put equal bets next to all three original bets. You can see how the stakes can grow fast in Multiple-Action Blackjack. If the dealer's up card is an ace, the player may take insurance (for up to half the bet) on any or all of his bets, or on none.

When it is the dealer's turn, he will deal another card next to his first card, and then play that hand in exactly the same way he would in standard blackjack. When the dealer has completed his hand, or busted, he will collect losing bets or pay off winning bets from the first of each players' circles. The dealer will then clear away all of his cards except the original up card. He will then move that card to the second rectangle and deal a second card onto it. This gives him a new hand, which he plays to completion. He will play his second hand and then collect bets or pay off bets from the players' second circles. The dealer then moves on to the third rectangle, playing a third hand starting with the same card.

It is possible, by the luck of the draw, to win all three bets or to lose all three bets for a big swing in bankroll. Or, it is also possible to win two and lose one, which, assuming equal bets, would be the equivalent of winning one bet on a standard blackjack table. (Of course, losing two while winning the third would be the equivalent of losing one bet.) With the ability to double down to a greater or lesser extent on different bets, a player might even manage to lose two of his three bets and still come out ahead overall. A dealer showing a 6 is in a bad position and it isn't very likely that he will draw 5s and then pull 21s on all three hands. (Unfortunately, you have to make your bets before you see the dealer's up card, so you're even more likely to get stuck with three bets against a dealer showing an ace.)

Multiple-Action Blackjack is a true gambler's game. It was made for the player who likes blackjack but wishes the stakes could get higher, with bigger swings in bankroll with each round of play. The odds are the same as standard blackjack, so, assuming you have enough money with you to cover the bets, there is no reason you should not play this game. It is more a matter of personal taste.

In the card-counting chapter of this book (Chapter 5), I will explain how Multiple-Action Blackjack can be used in the card counter's favor in really much the same manner as playing multiple hands of regular blackjack, which can be done on a fairly empty regular blackjack table. The game was probably invented by the casinos to increase the amount of money that could be bet in the same amount of time, as well as to entice gamblers who prefer a more exciting financial gamble. More money bet equals more money won for the casino.

BLACKJACK SIDE BETS

The side bet is another devious invention by casinos to increase the action at a blackjack table and to separate the players from their money. The side bet is similar to the blackjack bonuses you will find in various casinos (such as the ones used in Spanish 21), but the difference is that you must place a bet to receive the bonus.

At the table of a blackjack game with side bets, you will see a small circle to the side of each main bet circle. This is where the player can make the side bet. Usually, these bets have a minimum of just $1. In some cases, players can bet more than $1 and will be paid odds on whatever they bet. In other cases, the bet can only be made for $1. Before each round of blackjack, any player who wants to make the side bet will put his/her bet into the circle for the side bets. (In some cases, there are even slots built into the table where a player can insert a $1 chip. The table will even light up to show that the player has made the side bet. It is the perfect combination of the gameplay of blackjack, the action of craps, and the whistles and bells of the slot machine—Las Vegas at its finest.)

There are many different versions of side bets, but they usually involve matching a certain set of cards with your first two cards or with the dealer's up card. For example, a side bet called "Royal Match" will pay great odds to the player who gets a suited king and queen with his first two cards. In another bet, you may bet on whether the dealer's up card will be red or black. The odds on that bet are clear. You have a 50 percent chance of guessing correctly, obviously. The bet pays even odds, which would give neither the player nor the casino an edge. Unfortunately, if the dealer's up card is a two and you guess the correct color, the bet is called a push and you do not win. That small rule change gives the casino a greater than 3 percent edge.

The two side bets you are most likely to see in a casino these days are the "Over/Under" and the "Lucky 7s." The "Over/Under" is popular due to its simplicity and its constant action. It is extremely simple. The player must guess whether the total of his first two cards will be over or under 13. For example, 6♠ 3♥ is 9, which is under 13, while J♥ 9♣ is clearly over 13. For the over/under bet, an ace always counts as 1, not 11. The player can bet any amount from $1 to the set table maximum for the side bet. If the player guesses correctly, the bet will pay even odds. The bet provides constant action because for every single hand, the player can make the side bet and it will either be a winner or a loser. There is no waiting to hit a bonus or get lucky with the right combination of cards.

Hopefully, by now you have learned that the casinos will always throw in a rule or an exception that will give them the edge over the players. Have you spotted the casino's big edge in the Over/Under bet? Did you notice that a player can bet that his two cards add up to less than 13 or a player can bet that his two cards add up to more than 13, but a player can never bet that his two cards will add up to exactly 13? Much like the 0 and 00 spots on a roulette wheel, the two-card total of 13 is an instant win for the house. And because the over and under bets pay only even odds, the 13 gives the casino a giant edge, near 10 percent. An interesting point to note is that the over and under bets are not equally likely to happen (unlike the red/black bet or the heads/tails of a coin-flip). If you must make this side bet, you will lose less money by taking Over every time.

The "Lucky 7s" side bet is a bonus-type bet. The player will simply place a bet in the betting circle. There is no choice involved. Betting on the side bet simply makes the player eligible for the Lucky 7 bonuses. As the name implies, the player will earn bonuses for getting 7s in his hand. If the player's first card is a 7, he wins 3-to-

1 odds on his bet. If both of his first two cards are 7s, but they are different suits, he wins 50-to-1 odds. The odds go up to 100-to-1 if the two 7s are the same suit. Finally, if the player gets three 7s in a row, for a 21, he has hit the jackpot. A $5 bet will pay $2,500 for three unsuited 7s (500-to-1 odds), or $25,000 for a miraculous hand of three suited 7s (5,000-to-1 odds).

Obviously, those jackpots, no matter how rare, make the Lucky 7 side bet exciting. But they do not make the bet profitable. Even with those exceptional payoffs, your chances of hitting those bonuses are so low, they cannot recover all the losses that led up to that big hand. In fact, the overall edge on this side bet is more than 10 percent in the casino's favor. The jackpots are so tempting and the odds so hard to calculate correctly that players unknowingly play this side bet, when they would be better off simply leaving 10 percent of their money at the door.

CHAPTER THREE

BASIC BLACKJACK STRATEGY

If you read Chapter 1 of this book, or if you've played a lot of blackjack, then you know the rules of blackjack. That means you know *how* to hit, double, split, or surrender. But do you know *when* to do all those things? Although blackjack is a game of chance in which your winning or losing depends on which cards come up, there is a basic strategy you can follow that gives you the absolute best chance of winning. Perhaps you have heard that blackjack is a game with very good odds for the skilled player, as opposed to games of pure chance like roulette. The skilled player relies on basic strategy, which in turn relies on mathematics and probability, to make the right play in any situation.

Going back to our baseball game from Chapter 1, let's assume a new baseball player understands all the rules of baseball. He knows he can steal bases or stretch hits to doubles or triples. But, if he doesn't understand when an outfielder has to make a very long, hard throw, or what pitchers and catchers give him the best chance of successfully stealing, he will not be able to use the rules to his advantage. In fact, he may try stealing on a rocket-armed catcher who can throw him out every time.

In this chapter, you will learn basic blackjack strategy. You don't have to understand it, but you do have to have full faith that it works. You will have to memorize the charts in this chapter and know them cold. By following the strategy listed here, you will not yet be able to beat the casino, but you will be close.

LEARNING BASIC STRATEGY

To master basic strategy for blackjack, you need to know what the best action is for every possible situation. In other words, for whatever cards you have, given the one card of the dealer's that you can see, there is one action (hit, stand, double, split, etc.) that gives you the best chance of winning. I will now present to you every possible combination of your cards and the dealer's up card, and the corresponding strategy for that situation. It is your job to memorize them all.

Fortunately, the different situations can be grouped and, in most cases, the strategy can be understood with some basic common sense. Wherever possible, I will try to explain the reasoning behind the strategy without getting too deep into the math behind it. For each grouping, I will provide a chart showing the strategies for all corresponding card combinations. The charts provide an easy-to-memorize visual description of the strategies.

Note that this is the basic strategy for only one specific set of rules. In this case, I am providing the basic strategy for blackjack with the following rules: the dealer stands on soft 17, doubling is allowed after splitting, and the player can re-split hands

AT THE TABLE

Gamblers are superstitious people. There is no question about that. Most gamblers believe in luck and/or fate. They think that every time they roll those dice or ask for another card either the Gods of Luck will smile on them and they will win, or they will be forsaken and lose. And despite the arbitrary nature of luck (as anyone who has relied on it can attest), most gamblers also try their best to change their fates. Some wear lucky underwear, some carry lucky charms, and others rub their chips just the right way before betting.

But card counters are not gamblers, and this is an important point. Card counters do not rely on luck. Instead, card counters rely on mathematics, probability, and statistics. These, by the way, are much less fickle friends than Lady Luck. Sure, there will be days that you seem to win most of your hands or get really great cards every time, and there will be days that you can't seem to find a single blackjack. If you choose to think of this as luck, go right ahead. But remember that, as a skilled blackjack player you are playing for the long-term. And in the long-term, those good times and bad times will even out and, if you play correctly, you will finish on the winning end. Whether you have some good luck or some bad luck, it doesn't matter, because math is on your side.

Why am I telling you this now? I am about to show you the basic strategy for blackjack. It tells you the best action to take in every situation according to mathematics, not luck. If you play blackjack exactly as the basic strategy tells you to, you will maximize your chances of winning. If, however, you get a "hunch" or a "good feeling" and decide to hit that 13 against a 4, or just stand on 15 with the dealer showing 7, because you think it's about time the dealer busts, you might as well be throwing away your money. Yes, you might get it right once or twice, but, in the long run, you will certainly do worse than if you had simply followed basic strategy.

Back to those gamblers who will be sitting at the table with you. Sometimes these people let their superstitions affect all the other players at the table. You might hear things like "We all have to stand here and let the dealer bust," or "Don't take a card and wreck the flow of the cards," or other crazy ideas. As a non-gambler, you must be strong and ignore the "advice" or intimidation of these players. Superstitious players tend to get very angry when they feel another player has made an incorrect move. They think it hurts the karma at the table, or disrupts the way the cards will fall. Of course, this is nonsense. But a drunk, rowdy player who has seen nothing but "bad luck" can certainly wreck another player's good time.

When you are playing by basic strategy, you may make some moves that other players disagree with (like hitting a 12 against a 3)—especially when you are counting and adjusting your play according to the count. To reduce the chances of being noticed, try sitting at first base or in the middle of the table. Third base is the most watched seat, because it is the last player before the dealer. That means this player will often be choosing to either take a card for his own hand or leave the card for the dealer. If the player at third base takes a card that would have busted the dealer's hand, or passes on a card that then gives the dealer 21, he always gets blamed for the rest of the players' losses.

up to three times. In addition, there are slightly different strategies for playing one-or two-deck games and for playing multiple decks. Some strategies take into account what two cards the player has, to make up his hand, rather than just the total of the two cards. In other words, a 9♠ 7♣ might have a different strategy than a J♦ 6♠, even though both are hands of 16. The differences are slight, so in order to keep things easy to learn and remember, I will only discuss the hand total strategies.

Some casinos offer single-or double-deck blackjack, but even though the advantage is greater for the player in these games, it is more difficult to count them because they are dealt face down. It is also nearly impossible to back-count a single-deck game because there are fewer hands played per shuffle. These will be explained later. Therefore, I will focus on the strategy for six- and eight-deck games, but I will also explain the differences in strategies if you are playing a single-or double-deck game. Most of the blackjack tables you will find in Atlantic City and on the strip in Las Vegas will be six- and eight-deck games. Single- and double-deck blackjack is more prevalent in downtown Las Vegas and Reno casinos.

HOW TO READ THE CHARTS

Example:

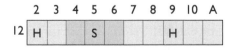

	2	3	4	5	6	7	8	9	10	A
12	H			S				H		

For each of the charts, the rows represent your cards and the columns represent the card the dealer is showing. In the

example above, we are looking at the one row that shows what you should do when your cards add up to 12. Across the top, you see the different possibilities for the dealer's up card, from two through ace. The "10" column represents all of the face cards and the ten, because these all have a value of 10. To determine the strategy for a specific combination, simply find the box (or area) where the corresponding row and column line up. In the charts, similar strategies are grouped together.

Looking at the chart above, if your cards add up to 12, you should stand (the "S") against any of the three cards 4, 5, or 6. You should hit ("H") with 12 against a 2 or 3 (the block at the left), or anything higher than a 6 (the block at the right).

Note that there will be separate charts for pairs and for soft hands. Therefore, if you see the number 8 in the left-hand column of a chart, it represents a hand of 3♥ 5♠ or 2♣ 6♦, but not 4♥ 4♦ (which will be represented as "4, 4"). Also, if you see the number 14, this represents a hard 14, such as 8♥ 6♣ or 2♦ 3♦ 4♦ 5♦ or A♠ 3♣ 10♦, but not A♥ 3♥ (which is a soft 14 and will be represented as "A3").

A general rule of thumb to remember when learning basic strategy (and when playing blackjack) is to assume that the next card will have a value of 10. This is not to say that the card will always be 10, or even that most of the time it will be 10, but it is still a useful assumption to make when thinking about how to play your hand. This is just based on the probabilities (see "Do the Math" on page 34).

This means that when thinking about what to do next, you should think as if taking a card will add 10 to your hand. That is why you will see that basic strategy tells you to double when you have 10 or 11 (because adding a 10 would give you hands of 20 or 21, respectively). It is also why you will stand in many cases when you have anything 12 or higher (because adding 10 would make your hand 22 or higher, and you would bust).

You should also assume that the dealer's hole card is a 10. This explains, for example, why you split almost any pair against a dealer showing a 6 (because you assume the dealer has a 10 in the hole, making his hand 16 and giving him a good chance of busting).

Do the Math

OK, it definitely makes it easier to understand basic strategy if you assume every card you can't see is a 10. But why would you do that, when it obviously isn't always true? Again, we go to good old mathematical probability.

There are 52 cards in a deck, four suits of 13 different cards. So there are 4 aces, 4 deuces, 4 threes, etc. But there are 4 tens, 4 jacks, 4 queens, and 4 kings, all of which count as 10. That makes 16 different cards in each deck that count as 10. That's about a 31 percent chance any one card will be a 10, or about 1 in 3. Obviously, that's much greater than the chance that the card will be any other single value (which is 4 in 52, or 7.7 percent).

Of course, if we knew that there was an even better than 31 percent chance that the next card would be a 10, basic strategy would be even more likely to work (since it is based on that one assumption). That is exactly what counting cards will do for you. When you count cards, you know when you have a better or worse chance of pulling a 10, and you can bet accordingly. For more on this topic, read Chapter 5.

WHEN TO HIT

Chart 1: Holding hard 5-8, unpaired

The very simple chart above describes the first and easiest rule of basic strategy. For any (unpaired, hard) hand that adds up to less than 9, you will always take a hit. It doesn't matter what the dealer has in this case.

The logic behind this strategy should be clear. When your hand is 8 or lower, you are in no danger of going over 21 when you hit, so you should always take one. In addition, you do not want to double because with a low hand, there is a good chance only one card will not be enough to make a good hand. For example, if you have a 3♥ 2♦ and double and get a 3♣, you are stuck with 8 (when, by the chart above, you should be taking another hit).

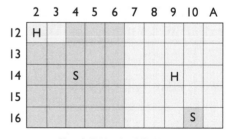

Chart 2: Holding hard 12-16, unpaired

The chart above shows that things get a little trickier when your hand adds up to anything between 12 and 16. In these cases, your action will depend on what the dealer is holding. The general rule is as follows: If the dealer shows a 6 or lower, stand; if the dealer shows a 7 or higher (including an ace), take a hit. As you can see from the chart, there are only three exceptions to that rule.

Remembering to assume any unseen card is a 10, we can see the logic behind the strategy. If you are holding anything over 11, taking a hit puts you in danger of busting. For example, even a low hand of 4♥ 8♣ would bust if a hit added a K♠ (4 + 8 + 10 = 22). Therefore, you have every right to be chicken, and not want to take another card. Luckily, the same problem occurs for the dealer, too. The dealer, however, doesn't have the choice to quit if his hand is lower than 17. So, assuming the dealer's hole card equals 10, the 2 through 6 across the top of Chart 2 represent dealer hands of 12 through 16. For any of these hands, the dealer will have to take a hit, and, assuming again that the card is a face card or a 10, the dealer will end up with a total of 22 through 26, respectively. The dealer busts and you win, even though you stopped with only 12.

Of course, when the dealer shows a 7 or higher, we assume he/she really has a hand of 17 or better. This obviously is good enough to beat us if we quit at 16 or less. Therefore, in those cases, you have to take a hit, even though probability says you will bust. (Basically, probability is reminding us of the old adage: you're damned if you do, and you're damned if you don't.) So, you should take a hit and hope for a small card that will not bust your hand.

The lower your hand is, the better chance you have of surviving your hit. Even though you always hear people at the table saying they hate hitting 12s more than anything else, you should definitely feel more confident hitting a 12 than a 16. After all, a 7, 8, or 9 bust a 16 but give a 12

a pretty nice hand. This brings us to the exception to the rule: If you have a 12 and the dealer has a 2 or a 3, you should take a hit. Because your chance of busting is low for a 12 and the dealer's chance of busting is also low for a 2 or 3 (think 12 or 13), the strategy changes for those hands.

The final exception occurs when you hold a 16 and the dealer is showing a 10. This is the worst possible combination for you, giving your lowest odds of winning the hand. In this case, rather than taking a hit in hopes of a miraculous five to beat a probable 20 for the dealer, you should just stand with 16 and hope the dealer doesn't have 20 after all. This is because the odds are high that you will bust if you take a hit, and that, even if you don't bust, your hand will still not be good enough to win. In other words, in this one case, the reward does not overcome the risk of taking a hit.

Note that you will see some basic strategies in other places that tell you to hit with 16 against a 10. The truth is that, with no knowledge about the cards or a count of 0, the choice is really a toss-up. You are just about equally likely to win whether you hit or stand. (And neither is very likely to win, I'm afraid.) Maybe this is why you will see so many people linger over this decision at the table and end up going with hunches. As you will learn in Chapter 8, you can use the count to decide what to do in this case, but for now, you should just stand every time.

Do the Math

I have told you that you must memorize the basic strategy and follow it exactly, without any deviations. In order to do that, you must have faith in the mathematics behind the strategy. So, to help you believe that these really are the best actions for each situation, let's go through a couple of easy ones so you can see where the strategies come from. I will go through all of the calculations that tell which action gives the best chance of winning.

Example 1: Player holds 14; dealer shows 6.

When you get a 14 and the dealer has a 6 showing, the correct strategy is to stand and hope the dealer busts. But how do we know that we shouldn't take a chance at improving the 14?

First of all, let's look at the dealer's hand. We know that the dealer has a 6, and we know exactly what the dealer will do (i.e., hit or stand) in every possible situation. Therefore, given the odds of any one card being in the hole for the dealer, or of any one card being the next one dealt, we can figure out the exact odds for the dealer's final hand. Once we know the odds for each hand the dealer will finish with, we can determine the odds that we will beat the dealer with our hand.

So what are the odds of any one card appearing next? For this example, we will take the simplest possible view of this. Let's assume that we will always be dealing from one complete deck. Of course, when we play, we know which cards have already been played and, therefore, which cards are more likely to come up next (i.e., the ones that have yet to be played). This is the basis of card counting. But for this example, let's not worry about the past and let's just assume each card is coming from a complete deck. Given that assumption, the chance of seeing each card are as follows:

Ace	4-out-of-52	7.69%
Two	4-out-of-52	7.69%
Three	4-out-of-52	7.69%
Four	4-out-of-52	7.69%
Five	4-out-of-52	7.69%
Six	4-out-of-52	7.69%
Seven	4-out-of-52	7.69%
Eight	4-out-of-52	7.69%
Nine	4-out-of-52	7.69%
Ten, Jack, Queen, King	16-out-of-52	30.77%

From those numbers, it follows that the odds of each hand the dealer may have with the first two cards are:

17 (Ace [11] + 6)	4-out-of-52	7.69%
8 (2 + 6)	4-out-of-52	7.69%
9 (3 + 6)	4-out-of-52	7.69%
10 (4 + 6)	4-out-of-52	7.69%
11 (5 + 6)	4-out-of-52	7.69%
12 (6 + 6)	4-out-of-52	7.69%
13 (7 + 6)	4-out-of-52	7.69%
14 (8 + 6)	4-out-of-52	7.69%
15 (9 + 6)	4-out-of-52	7.69%
16 (10 + 6)	16-out-of-52	30.77%

So we know that 7.69 percent of the time, a dealer showing a 6 will have an ace underneath, which makes 17. The dealer will stop there. (We are assuming here that the rules say the dealer stands on soft 17.) However, if any of the other cards comes up, by the rules the dealer must take a hit.

Using this simple methodology, we will use the same odds for the next card dealt. Let's take the example when the dealer had a 10 or face card underneath his 6, making a total of 16. The dealer will take another card, and the chances will look like this:

17 (Ace [1] + 16)	4-out-of-52	7.69%
18 (2 + 16)	4-out-of-52	7.69%
19 (3 + 16)	4-out-of-52	7.69%
20 (4 + 16)	4-out-of-52	7.69%
21 (5 + 16)	4-out-of-52	7.69%

22 (6 + 16)	4-out-of-52	7.69%
23 (7 + 16)	4-out-of-52	7.69%
24 (8 + 16)	4-out-of-52	7.69%
25 (9 + 16)	4-out-of-52	7.69%
26 (10 + 16)	16-out-of-52	30.77%

Adding up the odds for all of the over-21 hands, this translates to the following odds for final (three-card) hands when a dealer has 16 with the first two cards:

17	4-out-of-52	7.69%
18	4-out-of-52	7.69%
19	4-out-of-52	7.69%
20	4-out-of-52	7.69%
21	4-out-of-52	7.69%
BUST	32-out-of-52	61.54%

Starting with 16, the odds are easy, because the third card will always finish the dealer's hand. But now let's look at the case when the dealer holds 15 with his first two cards. The odds for the dealer's three-card totals are:

16 (Ace [1] + 15)	4-out-of-52	7.69%
17 (2 + 15)	4-out-of-52	7.69%
18 (3 + 15)	4-out-of-52	7.69%
19 (4 + 15)	4-out-of-52	7.69%
20 (5 + 15)	4-out-of-52	7.69%
21 (6 + 15)	4-out-of-52	7.69%
22 (7 + 15)	4-out-of-52	7.69%
23 (8 + 15)	4-out-of-52	7.69%
24 (9 + 15)	4-out-of-52	7.69%
25 (10 + 15)	16-out-of-52	30.77%

Notice that, while most of the time, the dealer will either complete his hand or bust, 7.69 percent of the time the dealer gets a 16 and must take a fourth card. We already know, from the calculations above, the odds of each final hand resulting from adding one card to a total of 16. (The number of cards used to make 16 doesn't matter, only the total.) To reiterate, when a dealer has 16 and takes another cards, the chances for each final hand are as follows: 17–7.69 percent, 18–7.69 percent, 19–7.69 percent, 20–7.69 percent, 21–7.69 percent, and bust 61.54 percent. When the dealer starts with 15, we know that there is a 7.69 percent chance he will get a 16 and have to take another card. To get the odds of the final hand starting with 15, we multiply the 7.69 percent by the odds of the final hands:

17	7.69% × 7.69% = 0.59%
18	7.69% × 7.69% = 0.59%
19	7.69% × 7.69% = 0.59%
20	7.69% × 7.69% = 0.59%
21	7.69% × 7.69% = 0.59%
BUST	7.69% × 61.54% = 4.73%

Now, we add these final-hand odds to the rest of the odds we found for the original starting total of 15, to find the overall chances of each final total:

17	7.69% + 0.59% = 8.28%
18	7.69% + 0.59% = 8.28%
19	7.69% + 0.59% = 8.28%
20	7.69% + 0.59% = 8.28%
21	7.69% + 0.59% = 8.28%
BUST	53.85% + 4.73% = 58.58%

As would be expected, when a dealer starts with 15 compared to 16, his chances of busting are lower (58.58 percent versus 61.54 percent) and his chances of finishing with any of the other hands go up (8.28 percent versus 7.69 percent). Yes, you are right to smile when the dealer flips over that hole card under the 6 and reveals a king.

Continuing our calculations, we can now find the odds of any final hand for a dealer whose two cards add up to 14. Again, we start with the familiar odds:

15 (Ace [1]+ 14)	4-out-of-52	7.69%
16 (2 + 14)	4-out-of-52	7.69%
17 (3 + 14)	4-outof-52	7.69%
18 (4 + 14)	4-out-of-52	7.69%
19 (5 + 14)	4-out-of-52	7.69%
20 (6 + 14)	4-out-of-52	7.69%
21 (7 + 14)	4-out-of-52	7.69%
22 (8 + 14)	4-out-of-52	7.69%
23 (9 + 14)	4-out-of-52	7.69%
24 (10 + 14)	16-out-of-52	30.77%

In this case, there are now two cards (ace and 2) that will force the dealer to take another card. We calculate the odds the same as before. Since we now know the final-hand odds for a dealer with 15 and a dealer with 16, we can again multiply those odds times the chance that a dealer who starts with 14 gets a 15 or a 16. The 7.69 percent chance that a dealer with 14 gets a 2 then breaks down as follows:

17	7.69% × 7.69% = 0.59%
18	7.69% × 7.69% = 0.59%
19	7.69% × 7.69% = 0.59%
20	7.69% × 7.69% = 0.59%
21	7.69% × 7.69% = 0.59%
BUST	7.69% × 61.54% = 4.73%

Notice that those odds are the same as were found for the 7.69 percent of the time when a dealer with a 15 in two cards gets an ace. The odds for the 7.69 percent of the time when the dealer's third card gives him 15 breaks down this way:

17	7.69% × 8.28% = 0.64%
18	7.69% × 8.28% = 0.64%
19	7.69% × 8.28% = 0.64%
20	7.69% × 8.28% = 0.64%
21	7.69% × 8.28% = 0.64%
BUST	7.69% × 58.58% = 4.51%

Adding all these percentages together gives us the odds of each finishing hand for the dealer that started with a two-card hand of 14:

17	7.69% + 0.59% + 0.64% = 8.92%
18	7.69% + 0.59% + 0.64% = 8.92%
19	7.69% + 0.59% + 0.64% = 8.92%
20	7.69% + 0.59% + 0.64% = 8.92%
21	7.69% + 0.59% + 0.64% = 8.92%
BUST	46.15% + 4.73% + 4.51%= 55.39%

We can continue this process for each possible two-card hand. When the dealer gets a 13 (again, a 7.69 percent chance), there is now a 7.69 percent chance he will get a 14 after three cards. Again, we multiply that 7.69 percent chance by the odds of final hands from a 14 that we just calculated:

17	7.69% × 8.92% = 0.69%
18	7.69% × 8.92% = 0.69%
19	7.69% × 8.92% = 0.69%
20	7.69% × 8.92% = 0.69%
21	7.69% × 8.92% = 0.69%
BUST	7.69% × 55.39% = 4.26%

Now, we can add up the odds for all final hands (for the dealer who started with a 13):

17	7.69% + 0.59% + 0.64% + 0.69% = 9.61%
18	7.69% + 0.59% + 0.64% + 0.69% = 9.61%
19	7.69% + 0.59% + 0.64% + 0.69% = 9.61%
20	7.69% + 0.59% + 0.64% + 0.69% = 9.61%
21	7.69% + 0.59% + 0.64% + 0.69% = 9.61%
BUST	38.46% + 4.73% + 4.51% + 4.26% = 51.96%

The calculations follow in the same way when a dealer gets a 6 to go with his first 6, for a two-card total of 12 (7.69 percent chance again). In that case, the 7.69 percent chance that the dealer's three-card total is 13 (6 + 6 + Ace) breaks down this way:

17	7.69% × 9.61% = 0.74%
18	7.69% × 9.61% = 0.74%
19	7.69% × 9.61% = 0.74%
20	7.69% × 9.61% = 0.74%
21	7.69% × 9.61% = 0.74%
BUST	7.69% × 51.96% = 4.00%

And the final odds are:

17	7.69% + 0.59% + 0.64% + 0.69% + 0.74% = 10.35%
18	7.69% + 0.59% + 0.64% + 0.69% + 0.74% = 10.35%
19	7.69% + 0.59% + 0.64% + 0.69% + 0.74% = 10.35%
20	7.69% + 0.59% + 0.64% + 0.69% + 0.74% = 10.35%
21	7.69% + 0.59% + 0.64% + 0.69% + 0.74% = 10.35%
BUST	30.77% + 4.73% + 4.51% + 4.26% + 4.00% = 48.27%

When the dealer turns over his hole card to reveal a 5 (for a total of 11), the three-card hand odds become:

12 (Ace [1] + 11)	4-out-of-52	7.69%
13 (2 + 11)	4-out-of-52	7.69%
14 (3 + 11)	4-out-of-52	7.69%
15 (4 + 11)	4-out-of-52	7.69%
16 (5 + 11)	4-out-of-52	7.69%
17 (6 + 11)	4-out-of-52	7.69%
18 (7 + 11)	4-out-of-52	7.69%
19 (8 + 11)	4-out-of-52	7.69%
20 (9 + 11)	4-out-of-52	7.69%
21 (10 + 11)	16-out-of-52	30.77%

Can you spot the big difference? With a total of 11, the dealer can't possibly bust on his third card. In fact, he has the greatest chance of pulling a ten-value card, for a 21. (Yes, it's right to moan when you see the dealer has a 5 in the hole to go with his 6.) However, because the dealer will still have to take another card for the 12 through 16 hands, there is still some chance he will bust. Again, we calculate the same way as before. The 7.69 percent chance of a 12 breaks down as follows:

17	7.69% × 10.35% = 0.80%
18	7.69% × 10.35% = 0.80%
19	7.69% × 10.35% = 0.80%
20	7.69% × 10.35% = 0.80%
21	7.69% × 10.35% = 0.80%
BUST	7.69% × 48.27% = 3.71%

Adding all the odds together, the chances of each final hand when starting with a two-card hand of 11 is:

17	7.69% + 3.45% = 11.14%
18	7.69% + 3.45% = 11.14%
19	7.69% + 3.45% = 11.14%
20	7.69% + 3.45% = 11.14%
21	30.77% + 3.45% = 34.22%
BUST	4.73% + 4.51% + 4.26% + 4.00% + 3.71% = 21.21%

When a dealer has a 4 under his 6, for a two-card total of 10, the odds are almost the same, but the chances are high for the dealer to pull a 20, rather than a 21 (because adding a ten-value card to the 10 gives 20). Again, the chances of busting come only when the dealer is forced to take a card with a 12 through 16. In fact, the final hand odds work out to:

17	7.69% + 3.45% = 11.14%
18	7.69% + 3.45% = 11.14%
19	7.69% + 3.45% = 11.14%
20	30.77% + 3.45% = 34.22%
21	7.69% + 3.45% = 11.14%
BUST	4.73% + 4.51% + 4.26% + 4.00% + 3.71% = 21.21%

When the dealer gets a 9 with two cards, the chances of a 21 go down because there is no way a third card can make a hand of 21. The only way the dealer can get 21 is to get an 11 through 16 with three cards, then make 21 on his fourth card (or beyond). However, the odds of a 19 go up because any of the ten-value cards makes a total of 19. The odds of busting, while still lower than before, go up because now the dealer must take an extra card for hands of 11 through 16 (versus 12 through 16 before). Therefore, adding up all of the odds, we get these final hand odds for a starting two-card hand of 9:

17	12.00%
18	12.00%
19	35.08%
20	12.00%
21	6.08%
BUST	22.84%

The odds occur similarly for a two-card hand of 8. In that case, the odds are highest that the dealer will finish with an 18, because of the high number of ten-value cards. There is also a better chance of the dealer getting a 17 (with a 9) or a 19 (with an Ace). The odds are lower of the dealer's getting a 20 or 21, because those totals require at least a fourth card. Again, the probability of busting goes up, because the dealer must take another card for hands from 10 through 16, not just 11

through 16. The final hand odds for a starting two-card hand of 10 are:

17	12.86%
18	35.93%
19	12.86%
20	6.94%
21	6.94%
BUST	24.47%

We have now calculated the probabilities of the dealer's final hand for every possible two-card hand (when the dealer is showing a 6). Those odds are shown in Chart 3, *on the next page*.

We already know the odds of the dealer having any of those two-card hands:

8	7.69%
9	7.69%
10	7.69%
11	7.69%
12	7.69%
13	7.69%
14	7.69%
15	7.69%
16	30.77%

Now, given Chart 3, *on the next page*, we can break down each of those two-card hand probabilities into its final-hand components, by multiplying by the odds that that two-card hand actually appears. For example, the odds of the dealer having a 2 in the hole, then making each of these final hands, add up to:

17	7.69% x 12.86% = 0.99%
18	7.69% x 35.93% = 2.76%
19	7.69% x 12.86% = 0.99%
20	7.69% x 6.94% = 0.53%
21	7.69% x 6.94% = 0.53%
BUST	7.69% x 24.47% = 1.88%

Dealer ends up with: →	17	18	19	20	21	BUST
Dealer's first two cards						
8 (6, 2)	12.86%	35.93%	12.86%	6.94%	6.94%	24.47%
9 (6, 3)	12.00%	12.00%	35.08%	12.00%	6.08%	22.84%
10 (6, 4)	11.14%	11.14%	11.14%	34.22%	11.14%	21.21%
11 (6, 5)	11.14%	11.14%	11.14%	11.14%	34.22%	21.21%
12 (6, 6)	10.35%	10.35%	10.35%	10.35%	10.35%	48.27%
13 (6, 7)	9.61%	9.61%	9.61%	9.61%	9.61%	51.96%
14 (6, 8)	8.92%	8.92%	8.92%	8.92%	8.92%	55.39%
15 (6, 9)	8.28%	8.28%	8.28%	8.28%	8.28%	58.58%
16 (6 plus 10, jack, queen or king)	7.69%	7.69%	7.69%	7.69%	7.69%	61.54%

Chart 3

Dealer ends up with: →	17	18	19	20	21	BUST
Hole card						
2	0.99%	2.76%	0.99%	0.53%	0.53%	1.88%
3	0.92%	0.92%	2.70%	0.92%	0.47%	1.76%
4	0.86%	0.86%	0.86%	2.63%	0.86%	1.63%
5	0.86%	0.86%	0.86%	0.86%	2.63%	1.63%
6	0.80%	0.80%	0.80%	0.80%	0.80%	3.71%
7	0.74%	0.74%	0.74%	0.74%	0.74%	4.00%
8	0.69%	0.69%	0.69%	0.69%	0.69%	4.26%
9	0.64%	0.64%	0.64%	0.64%	0.64%	4.51%
10	2.37%	2.37%	2.37%	2.37%	2.37%	18.93%
A	7.69%	0.00%	0.00%	0.00%	0.00%	0.00%

Chart 4

We can do the same for all possible hole cards. Doing so, we get Chart 4, *above*. The chart represents the actual probabilities of each of those final hands, based on only knowing the dealer's up card of 6.

By adding up the numbers for each column, we get the probabilities of the dealer's final hand, starting with only a 6 showing. These are the final probabilities:

17	16.54%
18	10.63%
19	10.63%
20	10.17%
21	9.72%
BUST	42.32%

We're now halfway to knowing our best strategy against a dealer showing a 6. The other half of the puzzle is knowing what the probabilities are that we will end up with a better or worse hand. To figure this out, we will follow the same process for our hand that we did for the dealer's hand.

It is a very simple problem if we choose to stand with 14. In that case, we know that we will lose to a dealer who ends up with a 17, 18, 19, 20, or 21, but we will win when the dealer busts. Of course, we just figured out the probabilities that the dealer will end up with those hands, so we now know our chances of winning if we stand. We win when the dealer busts, which will happen 42.32 percent of the time. We lose when the dealer makes any hand, which happens the rest of the time, or 57.68 percent. Put in monetary terms, it means that, in the long run, we will lose $15.36 for every $100 bet when standing with 14 against 6.

Lose $15.36 out of every $100 bet? That doesn't sound like a good bet, right? So why would we stand, rather than hitting? Well, let's take a look at the odds of our making a winning hand by hitting our 14.

Taking the same steps as we did before for the dealer's hand, let's look at the possible totals after we take our first hit:

15 (Ace [1] + 14	4-out-of-52	7.69%
16 (2 + 14)	4-out-of-52	7.69%
17 (3 + 14)	4-out-of-52	7.69%
18 (4 + 14)	4-out-of-52	7.69%
19 (5 + 14)	4-out-of-52	7.69%
20 (6 + 14)	4-out-of-52	7.69%
21 (7 + 14)	4-out-of-52	7.69%
22 (8 + 14)	4-out-of-52	7.69%
23 (9 + 14)	4-out-of-52	7.69%
24 (10 + 14)	16-out-of-52	30.77%

As you can see, there is a 46.15 percent chance that you will bust on your first hit to a 14. That is, of course, the big risk you take when you hit this hand. You also have a 15.38 percent chance of getting a hand below 17, so we will assume that you will want to take another hit on those hands.

Following the process just detailed above for the dealer's hand, we get these probabilities for your final hand when you hit with a 14:

17	8.92%
18	8.92%
19	8.92%
20	8.92%
21	8.92%
BUST	55.39%

You can see right away that if you take a hit you will automatically lose 55.39 percent of the time from going over 21. But, even in the cases when you get a 17 or better and don't bust, you are not guaranteed to win the hand. Using our chart of the dealer's probable finishing hands, we can figure out the exact probability that you will win or lose.

We know a 17 will be gotten 8.92 percent of the time. If you get a 17, the only way you can beat the dealer is if he busts. We know that will happen 42.32 percent of the time. You will tie with the dealer if he ends up with 17, as well. We know that will happen 16.54 percent of the time. The rest of the time (41.14 percent), unfortunately, your 17 is not good enough to win. That means, even if you manage to survive your hit to get a 17, you will still lose $1.18 for every $100 you bet.

What if you are lucky enough to end up with 18? Now you will beat the dealer who finishes with 17, as well as the dealer who busts. That means you win 58.86 percent (16.54 percent + 42.32 percent) of the time. You tie when the dealer ends up with 18, which will happen 10.63 percent of the time. You lose all the rest (30.51 percent). Finally, a winning hand. If you get an 18, you will win $28.35 for every $100. Unfortunately, you get that 18 just 8.92 percent of the time if you hit with a 14.

When you get:	17	18	19	20	21	BUST
You win	42.32%	58.86%	69.49%	80.11%	90.28%	0.00%
You tie	16.54%	10.63%	10.63%	10.17%	9.72%	0.00%
You lose	41.14%	30.51%	19.89%	9.72%	0.00%	100.00%

Chart 5

When you get:	17	18	19	20	21	BUST
You win	3.78%	5.25%	6.20%	7.15%	8.05%	0.00%
You tie	1.48%	0.95%	0.95%	0.91%	0.87%	0.00%
You lose	3.67%	2.72%	1.77%	0.87%	0.00%	55.39%

Chart 6

Making those calculations for every possible player's finishing hand, we get as shown in Chart 5, *above*.

If we multiply by the odds that you will achieve each of those hands, we get the following probabilities, indicated in Chart 6, *above*.

By adding the columns together for each row, we find the total odds of your winning or losing:

You Win	30.43%
You Push	5.16%
You Lose	64.42%

You can see that you will lose 55.39 percent of the time by busting and another 9.04 percent of the time by having a worse hand than the dealer's. In total, it means that for every $100 bet, you will lose $34.00.

Now compare that to your odds of winning when you stand with 14. You may not like losing $15.36 out of every $100 when you stand with 14 against 6, but it certainly beats losing $34.00, which is what you will do if you take a hit.

Therefore, according to the laws of probability, the correct action to take

when you have a 14 and the dealer shows a six is to stand. Which is exactly what basic strategy tells you to do.

Example 2: Player holds 14; dealer shows 7.

When the player holds a 14 and the dealer's up card is a 7 instead of a 6, the strategy changes. In that case, the player should hit rather than stand. Let's look again at the mathematics behind the strategy to see the difference.

Obviously, since the player has the exact same hand as in Example 1 above, the player (if he chooses to hit) will have the same final odds of making each hand:

17	8.92%
18	8.92%
19	8.92%
20	8.92%
21	8.92%
BUST	55.39%

There is still a 55.39 percent chance of losing the hand by busting and a further chance of losing when the dealer makes a higher hand. So how can this possibly be the best option? Let's look at the dealer's hand.

Dealer ends up with: →	17	18	19	20	21	BUST
Dealer's first two cards						
9	12.00%	12.00%	35.08%	12.00%	6.08%	22.84%
10	11.14%	11.14%	11.14%	34.22%	11.14%	21.21%
11	11.14%	11.14%	11.14%	11.14%	34.22%	21.21%
12	10.35%	10.35%	10.35%	10.35%	10.35%	48.27%
13	9.61%	9.61%	9.61%	9.61%	9.61%	51.96%
14	8.92%	8.92%	8.92%	8.92%	8.92%	55.39%
15	8.28%	8.28%	8.28%	8.28%	8.28%	58.58%
16	7.69%	7.69%	7.69%	7.69%	7.69%	61.54%

Chart 7

Dealer ends up with: →	17	18	19	20	21	BUST
Dealer's Hole card						
2	0.92%	0.92%	2.70%	0.92%	0.47%	1.76%
3	0.86%	0.86%	0.86%	2.63%	0.86%	1.63%
4	0.86%	0.86%	0.86%	0.86%	2.63%	1.63%
5	0.80%	0.80%	0.80%	0.80%	0.80%	3.71%
6	0.74%	0.74%	0.74%	0.74%	0.74%	4.00%
7	0.69%	0.69%	0.69%	0.69%	0.69%	4.26%
8	0.64%	0.64%	0.64%	0.64%	0.64%	4.51%
9	0.59%	0.59%	0.59%	0.59%	0.59%	4.73%
10, Jack, Queen or King	30.77%	0.00%	0.00%	0.00%	0.00%	0.00%
Ace	0.00%	7.69%	0.00%	0.00%	0.00%	0.00%

Chart 8

Instead of a 6, the dealer now has a 7 showing. This means that the dealer's two-card probabilities are the following:

18 (Ace [11] + 7)	4-out-of-52	7.69%
9 (2 + 7)	4-out-of-52	7.69%
10 (3 + 7)	4-out-of-52	7.69%
11 (4 + 7)	4-out-of-52	7.69%
12 (5 + 7)	4-out-of-52	7.69%
13 (6 + 7)	4-out-of-52	7.69%
14 (7 + 7)	4-out-of-52	7.69%
15 (8 + 7)	4-out-of-52	7.69%
16 (9 + 7)	4-out-of-52	7.69%
17 (10 + 7)	16-out-of-52	30.77%

Can you see why the dealer is in a much better position with a 7? Notice that the probability of the dealer having a finished hand with only two cards is now 38.46 percent. With a 6 showing, those odds were only 7.69 percent, and the extra hits led to a lot of busted hands for the dealer. Clearly, a dealer with a 7 showing will not bust as often.

In fact, since the rules we are playing are the same as in Example 1, the odds of any final dealer hand, given the same two-card starting hand, will be the same. Therefore, we can use these probabilities that we already found, indicated in Chart 7, *above*.

Note that we do not need a row for a two-card hand of 8 because there is no way a dealer with a 7 showing can make a two-card hand of 8. Now, if we multiply those percentages by the odds of each of those two-card hands occurring, we get the following final probabilities of each situation, as indicated in Chart 8, *on page 44.*

Again, by adding the rows for each column, we find the total probability of each final hand, given that the dealer is showing a 7. Those probabilities are shown here:

17	36.86%
18	13.78%
19	7.86%
20	7.86%
21	7.41%
BUST	26.23%

Compare these numbers to those for a dealer showing a 6. The dealer will now bust only 26.23 percent of the time, versus 42.32 percent with a 6 showing. Those numbers go straight to your bottom line.

If now, with a 7 showing, you were to stand with only 14, you would again lose every time the dealer makes a hand and win when the dealer busts. But by the numbers above, that means you will only win 26.23 percent of the time, losing 73.77 percent of the hands. That means you lose $47.54 for every $100 bet. That is so bad, it's barely better than surrendering (and automatically losing $50 out of every $100).

However, let's check the odds if we hit with 14 and take our chances. Our final hand odds will be the same as before:

17	8.92%
18	8.92%
19	8.92%
20	8.92%
21	8.92%
BUST	55.39%

Now, if we make a chart again of how often we will win or lose with each of those hands, we get Chart 9, *below.*

Again, even if you make a 17, you still lost $10.68 out of every $100 bet, but if you can make 18 or higher, you will win most of the time. Taking the odds listed above, we find the exact probabilities of each of these situations, shown in Chart 10, *below.*

Adding the columns for each row, we

When you get:	17	18	19	20	21	BUST
You win	26.23%	63.09%	76.87%	84.73%	92.59%	0.00%
You tie	36.86%	13.78%	7.86%	7.86%	7.41%	0.00%
You lose	36.91%	23.13%	15.27%	7.41%	0.00%	100.00%

Chart 9

When you get:	17	18	19	20	21	BUST
You win	2.34%	5.63%	6.86%	7.56%	8.26%	0.00%
You tie	3.29%	1.23%	0.70%	0.70%	0.66%	0.00%
You lose	3.29%	2.06%	1.36%	0.66%	0.00%	55.39%

Chart 10

get these final odds for winning against a dealer up card of 7 when you hit with 14:

You Win	30.65%
You Push	6.58%
You Lose	62.77%

Those are about the same odds as we had against a 6, but suddenly they look a lot more attractive. With these odds, you will lose $32.12 out of every $100 bet. Not good, but still a lot better than losing $47.54.

Therefore, as basic strategy tells you, when you hold a 14 and the dealer shows a 7, you should hit. Yes, you will lose more than you win, but you'll do better than you would have if you stayed at 14 and also better than if you surrendered.

Now, hopefully you have an appreciation of the mathematics behind the strategies and a little faith that these are the correct actions to take in each situation. Now, let's continue with another of the easiest charts you will ever have to memorize.

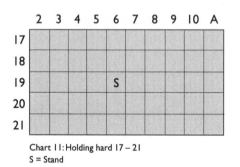

Chart 11: Holding hard 17 – 21
S = Stand

Chart 11 represents a very simple rule: If you have a hard 17 or higher, stand. It does not matter what the dealer holds. But I doubt you needed me to tell you to stand when you have 21. The logic behind this rule is obvious. Your hand is often good enough to win already, and more impor-

tantly, taking another hit would put you in grave danger of busting. Hitting an 18 in order to impress when you get a 3 should be left to those who drink their martinis shaken, not stirred, and carry a license to kill.

You will play an 18 differently if it is made up of a pair of 9s (see rules for splitting below), but you should always play a pair of 10s as a hard 20 and stand.

WHEN TO DOUBLE

There are only a few very specific cases when you should consider doubling. Most of these cases involve soft hands, when you get an ace in your first two cards. These cases will be covered later, in the section on how to play aces. The other cases occur when you have a total that is high enough to make a very good hand with only one more card, but not so high that you can bust with just one more card. Those totals are 9, 10, and 11. If you are observant, you were probably wondering why those hands were left out of the charts in the "When to Hit" section. They are shown in Chart 12, *below*. When you have a pair of 5s, you will always play them as a hard 10. You should never split 5s.

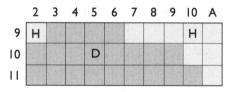

Chart 12: Holding hard 9 - 11
H = Hit
D = Double

The chart shows that when you have an 11 or a 10, you will double most of the time, but in all cases, it depends on the dealer's up card. If you have an 11, you should double against any card except for an ace. With an 11, you should expect to have a very good hand after taking one card. Many times, you will get a 10 or face card, for the unbeatable total of 21. Even if you do not score a 21, you will possibly get a 7, 8, or 9, for a hand of 18 or more.

Of course, if we assume that our next card will be a 10, there is nothing the dealer can get that will beat our 21. However, when the dealer holds an ace, we cannot take the risk. Even assuming the dealer doesn't have blackjack (which you will usually know before you have to decide to double), the ace gives the dealer extra flexibility and less chance of busting, and therefore, greater chance of beating your hand if you don't get the 21. For that reason, you should merely take a hit when the dealer has an ace. A lot of the time, you will still take only one card, but you will save the extra bet in those times when the dealer pulls something to beat you.

The rule for when to double with 10 follows the rule for doubling with 11. You should double against any card that you can expect to beat if the next cards are all 10s. Therefore, with a total of 10 in your first two cards, double against a dealer showing anything up to a 9. Against a 10 or an ace, you should simply take a hit.

When you have a total of 9 with your first two cards, you are not in as strong a position. The 10 we expect only gives you a hand of 19. This is good, but not an unbeatable 21, to be sure. Besides 10s and aces, only a 9 gives you a hand with a chance to beat a dealer that doesn't bust. (If the dealer doesn't bust, he will always have 17 or more. That means you will need 18 or more to win the hand.) In addition, take the following example: You

hold 5♣ 4♣ and the dealer has a 7♥. You take a hit and your next card is 2♠. In this case, hitting rather than doubling gave you the chance to hit the strong hand of 11 (5 + 4 + 2 = 11) you have now, rather than be stuck with a doubled bet and a hand of 11.

This is the reason we double with 9 *only* when the dealer has a weak hand. To be exact, when you hold 9, you should double only against a dealer's card of 3 through 6. As we have already discussed, when the dealer shows a 6 or lower, we expect him to bust, so it is worth a chance to double your win when he does. A dealer showing a 2 is a little more dangerous. Even if the next card dealt is a 10, the dealer will then hold a 12 and still have a pretty good chance to draw another card without busting. (Only a 10 or face card will bust a 12.) For this reason, do not double with 9 against a 2.

Here is one example of the number of decks making a difference in the strategy. When playing a six- or eight-deck game, as I just said above, you will double with a 10 against any dealer up card from 2 to 9. However, when playing a one- or two-deck game, you should not double with 10 against a 9. You will only double against a dealer card up to 8. The difference is small, and, in fact, when you read about counting cards and changing your strategy based on the count, you will see that some decisions are easily swayed by the cards that have already been played. This is one of those decisions, and if the count goes up the smallest amount, it is actually a better play to double, even in a single- or double-deck game. The chart for doubling strategy in single-and double-deck games is shown on the following page.

AT THE TABLE

Here is another warning about dealers taking charge of your game. When you hit a small hand and get another small card, you will often find that the dealer just automatically gives you another card, usually before you even signal for a hit. It usually catches an inexperienced player by surprise. While he struggles to add up the cards he had, the dealer starts adding more cards.

There really isn't anything wrong with the dealer doing this. Dealers generally won't do it unless the hand is clearly in need of a hit and can't go bust. And hopefully you will put in enough practice at home and in the casino to be able to count your hand total (and also keep the running count) fast enough to not be taken by surprise. Nonetheless, if it bothers you when a dealer acts without your express direction, just tell him and he won't do it again.

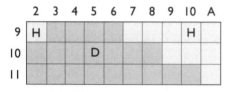

	2	3	4	5	6	7	8	9	10	A
9	H								H	
10				D						
11										

Chart 13: Holding hard 9-11, one- or two-deck game
D = Double
H = Hit

In all of the cases above, you can double only when your first two cards make the totals listed. For example, if you have a 3♥ 4♦ 4♣, for 11, by the rules you can't double. In this case, you should simply take a hit. You can't bust with another card, and you can't beat the dealer if he doesn't bust, so you should obviously take a hit.

WHEN TO SPLIT

A pair can be a very valuable hand. It can be split, re-split, and doubled, to create a powerful hand worth much more money than you originally bet. Splitting can even, in the case of a pair of 7s or 8s, turn one bad hand (a 14 or 16, respectively) into two good hands. In fact, if you play your pairs correctly, you will find that winnings on split hands give you the edge to cover losses on all those 15s and 16s you had to

hit against the dealer's 7 (and all those other losses, too).

The strategy chart for playing pairs is below. Notice that pairs of 5s (5, 5) and 10s (10, 10) do not appear on the chart. That is because, as stated in earlier sections, you should always play a pair of 5s as a 10 and pair of 10s as 20. You will find the strategies for a pair of 5s (10) in Chart 12 *(page 46)* and for a pair of 10s (20) in Chart 11 *(page 46)*.

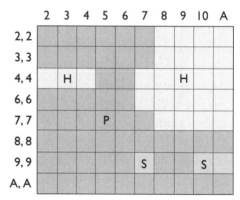

	2	3	4	5	6	7	8	9	10	A
2, 2										
3, 3										
4, 4		H						H		
6, 6										
7, 7				P						
8, 8										
9, 9						S			S	
A, A										

Chart 14: Holding a pair
H = Hit
P = Split
D = Double

To understand the strategies for pairs, let's start at the bottom of Chart 14. When you have a pair of aces, there is only one thing to do: split them and hope for 10s. There is a good chance you will get two 10s or face cards, leaving you with two unbeatable hands of 21. If you don't get two, you have a very good chance of getting one 21, and even if you don't get a 10 on the other hand, you will probably do no worse than a push. *Example:* You bet $10 and get A♥ A♣. You put down another $10 and split. You get a K♠ on one hand for 21 (A♥ K♠), but on the other hand you get a 3♣ for 14 (A♣ 3♣). Remember, you only get one card when you split aces. The dealer had a 10♦ and draws a J♣, for 20. You win $10 on your first hand (21 beats 20) but you lose $10 on your second hand (20 beats 14), so you come out even—a push. Therefore, it is always a good idea to split aces.

When you have a pair of 9s, you already have 18, which is a reasonably good hand. However, if you split, you can make two good hands out of it and win twice as much money. You will always want to split 9s when the dealer has a 6 or lower, because you are expecting the dealer to bust. Therefore, you should take the chance to double your money when the dealer busts.

When the dealer shows a 7, we are going to assume that the dealer will draw a 10 for a total of 17. A pair of 9s makes 18, which beats 17, so rather than taking a chance at making two hands that will beat 17, you should stand with the safe 18 that already can beat the dealer. When the dealer shows an 8 or 9, you are assuming he will end up with hands that can tie or beat your 18. However, if you split your 9s and get 10s or face cards on both, you will have two 19s, which will beat or tie the dealer's expected hand. Note that even though a 19 would only tie the dealer with a 9 showing, you should try it, rather than sitting on an 18 that would be a loser. Obviously, it is better to push two hands than lose one.

Finally, when the dealer has a 10 or ace showing, it is not worth the risk to bet more. Even if you were to give up your 18, and you got two 10s, you would still only have two 19s, which wouldn't beat the dealer's expected hand. Therefore, it is best to stand with a pair of 9s against a 10 or ace and hope for the best. At worst, you will only lose one bet and not two.

The rule for playing a pair of 8s is a simple one: always split 8s. Unlike aces, however, it isn't because you have such a strong hand. Instead, it is because you have such a poor hand. Without splitting, you would have to play the two 8s as a total of 16, which is the worst hand you can have. When the dealer shows a 6 or lower, you will still be splitting because you expect the dealer to bust. But when the dealer shows a 7 or higher, you should split because it is a bad play to hit or to stand. If you were to hit, you would be very likely to bust. If you were to stand with 16, any dealer hand that doesn't bust would beat you. Therefore, you should take your chances and split in hopes of improving your hand. If the dealer shows a 7 or 8, you are expected to beat the dealer or at least tie. If, however, the dealer has a 9, 10, or ace, you should just hope for the best. Often, you will pull two 10s and still lose when the dealer gets a 19 or 20. But your 16 would have lost, too, so take the chance.

Pairs of 2s, 3s, 6s, and 7s are not very good hands by themselves. The totals of 4, 6, 12, and 14 aren't exactly world-beaters. Unfortunately, splitting these hands isn't guaranteed to do you much better, because the cards are so low. Therefore, you should only split these pairs against low dealer cards. Like the pairs already discussed, you should split these pairs against any dealer card of 6 or lower, expecting the dealer to bust. In the case of 2s, 3s, and 7s, you will also split the hand against a 7. A pair of 7s is 14, but when split has a good chance to make two 17s. That should be good enough for a push against a dealer 17. In the case of 2s and 3s, because you will be starting with a low card, there is a very good chance that at least one of your hands will be able to beat the dealer in the end. Therefore, you have a very good chance at a push or better, so you should split. A pair of 6s, however, is not good enough to split against a 7. You are likely to get a pair of 16s, which are likely then to become two busted hands against a 7 or higher (because you will have to hit them to try to beat the dealer).

Against a dealer showing an 8 or higher, you will play these pairs just like hard hands. You should hit and hope for the best.

A pair of 4s is an interesting case, because when split, 4s do not make very impressive beginnings to hands, but when kept together, they make 8, which can be a good start to a hand. Therefore, you will split 4s less than other hands. In fact, you should only split 4s against a dealer showing 5 or 6. Those are the two dealer hands most likely to bust, and therefore worth giving up the 8 for the chance at double the winnings. In all other cases, you should just hit the 8 and hope for a 10 or ace to make a hand of 18 or 19.

When playing at a single- or double-deck blackjack table, there is one small difference in the splitting strategies. When you hold a pair of 7s, basic strategy for multiple decks tells you to split against any dealer up card from 2 to 7. Basic strategy for single-and double-deck games tells you to go one further, and split your 7s even against an 8. Again, this is a decision that is very close to a toss-up. It is just about equally valuable to split as to hit against a dealer with an 8, and will really depend on the running count at the time of the decision. The splitting chart for single and double-deck blackjack is shown below.

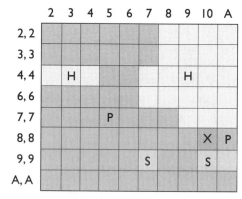

Chart 15: Holding a pair, one- or two-deck games
X = Surrender
P = Split
H = Hit
S = Stand

Splitting pairs at the right time not only makes you look smart, it will make you money. If nothing else, pairs are certainly the most fun hands you will get. Nothing beats the excitement of splitting and re-splitting and doubling those hands. Except maybe a blackjack on a big bet.

PLAYING ACES

Aces make for very powerful hands, because of their flexibility. Soft hands (that is, hands in which the ace can still count as either 1 or 11) give you great security because there is no card in the deck that can bust your hand. That is why, when you have a soft hand, you will almost always take a card. Unless your hand is already very good (like an A8 or A9), you can always take a card and see if you can make your hand better, without any fear of busting. Soft hands made up of only two cards are even more powerful because, with that free card that can't bust you, you can double your bet when the dealer has a good chance of busting himself. A win isn't guaranteed, but you will definitely win a greater percentage of your hands when you have an ace.

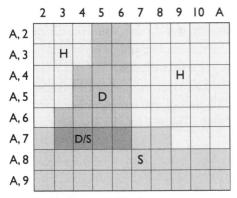

	2	3	4	5	6	7	8	9	10	A
A, 2										
A, 3		H								
A, 4								H		
A, 5				D						
A, 6										
A, 7			D/S							
A, 8						S				
A, 9										

Chart 16: Holding a soft hand
H = Hit
D = Double
S = Stand
DS = Double, or Stand if you cannot double

Let's start with the easy hands. Let's say you have an ace and an eight or nine. Congratulations, you have a great hand. Stop there and be satisfied that you will probably win. You don't ever hit (or double) with an A8 or A9, because you're not going to get a better hand. You have a 19 or a 20. Don't get greedy. (If you are wondering whether to hit an A10, I suggest you take up a different hobby. You have 21. You can't lose!)

Now look closely at the hands A2 through A7 in Chart 16. Do you see a pattern? You should be able to tell with just a glance, that as your hand gets higher, you will double more often. Why is that? Put simply, the lower hands have a better chance at making a good hand with multiple hits and, therefore, it isn't worth the risk of doubling your money and only getting one card.

Example: You get an A♣ 2♠. You double, and your next card is a J♠. You're now stuck with a 13. Your only hope is for the dealer to bust. Now, let's go back to that same A♣ 2♠, but this time you just take a hit. You get the same J♦, for 13. Now, you can hit it again. You draw an 8♣. Voilà! A 21.

As your hand gets higher, you are less likely to take multiple hits and draw a good hand, and so it becomes worth risking the double for only one hit. Of course, this risk becomes safer as the dealer's card gets higher, because that means an increased chance that the dealer will bust. That is why the strategy tells you to double A2 through A7 against a 5 or 6, but only A4 through A7 against a 4, and only A6 or A7 against a 3. There is no easy way to think about why the strategy changes for each of those specific cards. You will just have to memorize the pattern.

Of course, the same rules for doubling apply, whether you have an ace or not. That means that you will only be able to double when you get A5 (or whatever hand) on your first two cards. In other words, with A♦ 5♣, you can double against a 4♥, but with A♦ 3♣ 2♣ (which also counts as a soft 16, or A5,) you cannot double. In most cases, just as you learned in When To Double on *page 46*, you will hit when you aren't allowed to double. You are holding a soft hand with an ace, so you cannot possibly bust. Therefore, take a hit and see what you get. It can't hurt, right?

Or can it? Take a look at the row next to A7. Notice that rather than just "D," it says "D/S." That means that when you can't double, because the 7 is made up of more than one card, you should stand rather than hit. The reason is that an A7 is an 18, which is not such a bad hand. It's not so good that it isn't worth the risk sometimes to double your money, but it's also not so bad that you absolutely need to try to make it better. The strategy shows that for an A7, in fact, you will only ever take a hit when you can double against a bad dealer hand, or when the dealer has a card that's good enough to beat your 18. That means when the dealer shows a 9, 10, or ace (which, as I'm sure you're tired of hearing by now, we will assume becomes a 19, 20, or 21, respectively). When the dealer has one of those cards, you will take a hit, hoping to get a small card to put yourself over the expected dealer hand. For all the other hands, you should just stand with 18, and you have a good chance of winning.

WHEN TO SURRENDER

In the sections above, for simplicity's sake, I have intentionally neglected to mention a few key cases where the strategy deviates from the usual. These are the few times when it is actually better for you to give up half your money and not even try to win the hand—in other words, the times you should surrender. There aren't many of them (thankfully), but if you play them correctly, you will save yourself a lot of money. As I've said already, the surrender rule is the most valuable rule in blackjack to a player who uses it at the right time.

In Chart 2 (*page 34*), I showed you the following for hard 15 and hard 16:

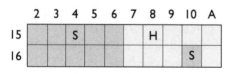

	2	3	4	5	6	7	8	9	10	A
15			S				H			
16									S	

Chart 17: Holding hard 15 or 16

I also told you that when you have a 16 against a 10, you should just stand rather than hoping for a miracle. Well, the truth is that, rather than hitting in hopes of that

miracle 5 and rather than standing and waiting for the dealer to turn over the other 10 and take all your money, you should surrender. That way, at least you keep half of your bet. In fact, a 16 is such a bad hand for you, you should not only surrender when the dealer shows a 10, but also when the dealer shows a 9 or an ace. In those cases, the chances that your hit will bust you (or that even if it doesn't, you will still lose) are so high, it is safer and more lucrative in the long run to surrender half your bet. You should also surrender with a 15 against a 10.

Therefore, the strategy chart for a hard 15 and 16 actually looks like this:

	2	3	4	5	6	7	8	9	10	A
15			S				H		X	H
16								X	X/S	X

Chart 18: Holding hard 15 or 16 (with surrender)

In the chart above, "X" represents surrender. If you cannot surrender, because the casino where you are playing does not provide that rule, then you should just hit (and think about playing at a different casino.) In the space for a 16 against a 10, the "X/S" means that you should surrender, or, if you aren't allowed, just stand.

There is one more case where it makes sense to surrender. That is when you hold a pair of 8s (for the dreaded 16) and the dealer shows a 10. If you can, you should surrender rather than splitting and hoping to get two big hands and then still having to get lucky to win. So, the chart for a pair of 8s looks like this:

	2	3	4	5	6	7	8	9	10	A
8, 8				P					X/P	

Chart 19: Holding a pair of 8's (with surrender)

AT THE TABLE

You may have heard the quote: "It is better to die on your feet than live on your knees." It was no doubt first spoken by someone who would never surrender in blackjack. But, believe me, it takes courage and determination to surrender. You will be ridiculed and insulted for doing it. Especially if you are at a low-stakes table, the dealer may comment at your cowardliness ("I'd hate to go into battle with this guy") or perhaps your parsimony ("Congratulations, you saved $2.50"). Oh, he'll get a good laugh out of the other people at the table (who didn't even know there was such a rule as surrender), but you must stand your ground. You are only doing what is best in the long run, and you may have only saved a small amount on that hand, but, in the long run, that money will add up. Surrendering just twice when you would have lost otherwise saves you one bet, and if that amount is so small you can throw it away, maybe you should move up to the high-stakes table.

So don't be afraid to surrender. Say it loud and say it proud, and you'll get the last laugh, when the dealer turns out to have 20 and everyone else loses.

You should split a pair of 8s against any dealer card except a 10 or face card. In that case, you should surrender. If you are not allowed to surrender, then you should split against a 10 as well.

WHEN TO TAKE INSURANCE

There is a very simple answer to the question of when to take insurance: Never. It is just not worth the risk to protect your hand for the few times the dealer will have blackjack.

Do the Math

Think of it this way: The dealer is showing an ace, and taking insurance is the same as betting (with 2-to-1 odds) that the card underneath the ace is a 10 or face card. In order to make that bet worthwhile, the chance that the card is a 10 or face card would have to be better than the odds, or, in this case, better than a 1-in-3 chance. However, assuming we know nothing about cards already played, there are 12 face cards and 4 tens in a deck, and 36 other cards. If you bet $1 on insurance 52 times, you would win 16 times and lose 36 times. With the odds, you would win $32 (sixteen $1 bets at 2:1 odds) but you would lose $36, so you come out negative $4. Rather than a 1-in-3 chance of the dealer having blackjack, there is a 1-in-3.25 chance. This makes insurance a losing bet.

Do not be tempted by "even money" when you have a blackjack. Just because you have a blackjack, the odds of the dealer also having blackjack do not change. Yes, it feels bad to only get a push when you have a blackjack, and that will happen, but you must remember that the odds do not change and, in the long run, you will win more money from the blackjack bonuses you did not forfeit by taking "even money" than the money you feel you'll lose on dealer blackjacks. (Remember that you don't actually lose any money when both you and the dealer have blackjacks.)

PRACTICE THE BASIC BLACKJACK STRATEGY

I have already said it several times, but I'll say it again. You must memorize basic blackjack strategy. You should study it well, until you can recall the specific action for any situation quickly and automatically. It won't do you any good to count cards and bet high when you have the advantage, if you make basic strategy mistakes (and hand that advantage back to the casino).

What is the best way to learn basic strategy? Well, you may want to think back to your school days, and just use whatever system worked best for you then. Maybe you want to just study the charts for hours, or re-read this chapter time after time, until you have soaked up the information.

If you learn better by testing yourself, flash cards may be the best method. Pick some of the trickiest situations, like 4, 4 against 4 or A7 against 8 or 12 against 3. Write the situation—your hand and the dealer's up card—on one side of an index card and write the correct action on the other side. Then guess the correct action for each situation and go through all the cards as many times as necessary until you can always guess correctly.

Some people learn best when they write information down. If you are one of those people who had to copy his notes three times before every test, you should try the same thing here. Put away the book and get a piece of paper. Now try to re-create the basic strategy charts exactly as shown in this chapter. Obviously, if you can duplicate the charts perfectly, it means you have memorized basic strategy. However, just because you have memorized it doesn't mean you'll be able to recall it quickly, especially when under pressure from the dealer and fellow players to make your move. Make sure to keep re-creating the strategy charts until you can do it quickly and easily (and without any errors).

Any of those methods could work, and they're probably your best bets for memorizing the material quickly and accurately. But they're not much fun, and they also won't help you make quick decisions in a real black-jack game. For that, you will want to practice with the real thing: playing blackjack.

You can learn a lot from good blackjack software for your computer. Not only will you be able to play many hands of blackjack quickly in the comfort of your own home, but most blackjack software also includes basic strategy help. You will be able to set your computer program to offer you tips on the correct move to make, or to alert you when you make an incorrect move. Just be sure to check the strategy charts that the computer is using. (You should be able to find an option that allows you to view the strategy charts, and even to make changes to them.) Make sure that the strategy your computer is using matches exactly to the strategy I've given you here.

Now, just play as many blackjack hands as you can, and think about the correct action according to basic strategy before you make your move each time. Then, either check the chart after making your move to see if you are correct, or set the computer to tell you when you've made the wrong move. In this way, you will learn from experience which actions to take and when to take them, and in time you will know the basic strategy cold (and also know which decisions you are more likely to face than others).

Of course, the best thing about playing blackjack on your computer instead of at the casino is that you can't lose real money. But, if you're dying to get to a casino and put your new blackjack knowledge to work, you can also practice basic strategy at a real casino. If you follow basic blackjack strategy perfectly, you will cut the casino's edge to less than 1 percent. So you won't avoid losing money, but if you don't bet too high, it won't cost you too much to get some real-life authentic casino blackjack experience.

Casino managers understand the numbers and they know that even with perfect basic strategy, a player will still lose money. So they have no problem with a player using strategy aids at the table. Therefore, you should bring the strategy charts with you to the casino and keep them handy. (Don't worry, you will not be the only person in the casino looking at the charts.) Before you make your move at the table, check your chart and make sure you are going to make the right action for the situation. (Check before you make your move, because you're playing for real money now.) You will probably want to play low stakes because you do not want to lose much money and you do not want the other players at the table getting frustrated with your slow decision-making. (They still might get frustrated, but if they're at a low-stakes table, they're more likely to also be beginners and, therefore, more understanding.)

If you choose to learn basic strategy by playing blackjack, make sure you play *a lot* of hands before declaring yourself an expert. There are many different card combinations, so the odds of your actually being faced with any one specific situation are extremely low. That means you will have to play many hands of blackjack to face all the different situations you need to memorize (or at least to see several varying situations). In fact, you may see a few situations only rarely, so you should still augment this type of practice with some of the more conventional strategies, to make sure that you really know the entire basic strategy chart perfectly.

To make it a little easier on you for studying purposes, I've condensed all of the charts and included the complete basic strategy in Appendix B, on *page 108*. The complete basic strategy for single- and double-deck games is provided in Appendix F, on *page 116*.

REVIEW QUESTIONS

For the following questions, assume that you are playing blackjack with the baseline rule set: The dealer stands on all 17s; splitting is allowed up to three times; doubling is allowed after splitting; and late surrender is offered. For each question, I will give you the player's hand, as well as the dealer's up card. Based on just those cards, you should be able to say the best action for the player to take on his turn, according to basic strategy. (New readers may want to look back at the charts in this chapter to find the right strategy, but in time you should be able to answer all of these questions from memory.)

1. Player: Q♥ 7♦   Dealer: 3♥
2. Player: 2♣ 3♣   Dealer: K♥
3. Player: 9♠ 3♥ 6♠   Dealer: 6♣
4. Player: 6♦ 5♠   Dealer: J♦
5. Player: 4♥ 5♣   Dealer: 2♠
6. Player: 2♦ 8♥   Dealer: A♦
7. Player: 5♠ 5♥   Dealer: 6♣
8. Player: 7♣ 7♦   Dealer: 4♦
9. Player: 9♥ 9♣   Dealer: 7♠
10. Player: 8♣ 8♠   Dealer: Q♥
11. Player: A♣ 2♦   Dealer: 4♥
12. Player: A♥ 4♠ 3♣   Dealer: 2♣

CHAPTER FOUR

RULE VARIATIONS

If you have finished reading through the entire basic strategy described in the last chapter, and you have studied hard and memorized all of the charts, congratulations. Now I have some bad news for you. The strategy you should play is not the same for every blackjack game you will ever play. Not every casino plays by the same rules. I mentioned in Chapter 1 that there are various house rules casinos use to increase their edge, or to attract customers by lowering their edge.

For each set of blackjack rules, there is a different basic strategy. Because the rules affect how the hands will play out, or the value of splitting versus doubling versus just hitting, you may want to do different things based on what you will be allowed to do with that hand (or on the rules the dealers play by). Luckily, the differences are not too great. If a casino does not allow you to double on your resultant hands after you split a pair, your strategy will tell you to split less often, but this will only affect your play on pairs and not any other hands.

What I have given you for the basic strategy is a strategy based on one specific set of rules. This basic strategy is valuable, however, because it represents the rules at the majority of the casinos you will play. (These are somewhat standard rules for Las Vegas strip casinos, but you may find tougher rules at smaller Indian casinos or casinos that face less competition than Las Vegas casinos.) The rules this basic strategy were based on are: Dealer stands on soft 17; splitting isallowed on any two cards; doubling is allowed after splits; hands can be re-split up to three times, except for aces, which cannot be re-split.

WHEN THE DEALER HITS SOFT 17

One of the most frequent aberrations from this set rule you will see is dealers hitting soft 17s. You will find that many casinos, even in popular casinos in Las Vegas, use this rule. Sadly, this is the single best rule for the casino; it adds the most to the casino's advantage. I will tell you later how to account for this and other rules when choosing your bet according to the count. But you should probably also know the changes to make to your basic strategy given this rule.

As you would expect, most changes to basic strategy occur when the dealer is showing an ace. Those are the cases when there is the best chance that the dealer will get a soft 17. Because this rule helps the dealer, making it more likely that the dealer gets a good hand, you will have to surrender more hands. Specifically, you should surrender a pair of eights against an ace, rather than splitting. (Of course, you should still split the hand if you are not allowed to surrender.) The strategy chart for pairs, when dealers hit soft 17, is provided on the next page.

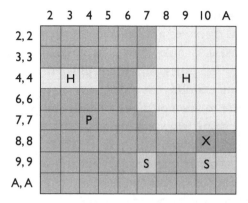

Chart 20: Holding a pair, dealer hits soft 17
H = Hit
P = Split
X = Surrender
S = Stand

You should also surrender a 15 against an ace if the dealer hits on soft 17. You were already surrendering 15 against a 10, as well as 16 against 9, 10, or ace. But when the dealer hits soft 17s, you should surrender the 15 against the ace, as well. In fact, you should also even surrender a 17 against an ace. When the dealer hits soft 17s, the chances that the dealer ends up with a total of 17 are lowered, which makes any 17 you have less valuable. It is so low-value that it makes more sense to give up half your bet than to sit with a 17 and hope for a push. Obviously, when you cannot surrender, you should stand with 17. The new strategy chart for hard 12 through 17 is included below.

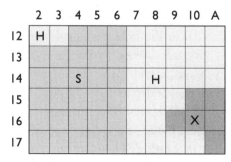

Chart 21: Holding hard 12-17, dealer hits soft 17

Finally, there are two cases where you should double where you would have only hit if the dealer stands on soft 17. The first is when you have 11 and the dealer shows an ace. That means that, when the dealer hits on soft 17s, you should always double with 11. If you cannot double, you should just hit your 11, like you would when the dealer stands on all 17s. In addition, you will break the rule that you always stand with a soft 19 (i.e., ace and 8). When you have a soft 19 and the dealer has a 6, you should double. If you cannot double, you should stand with 19. The strategy chart for soft hands when dealers hit soft 17 is shown below.

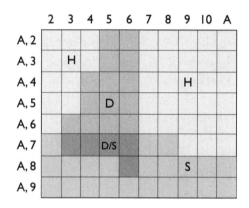

Chart 22: Holding soft hand, dealer hits soft 17
H = Hit
D = Double
S = Stand
D/S = Double, or Stand if you cannot double

To make it easier for you, the complete basic strategy when the dealer hits soft 17s is provided at the end of the book, Appendix C, on *pages 110 and 111*.

WHEN YOU CANNOT DOUBLE AFTER SPLITTING

It makes perfect sense that if you are playing in a casino that does not allow doubling after splits, you will not split as often. Splitting just isn't as valuable if you won't be able to double your money when you end up with a

10 or 11 on one or both of your hands. For that reason, it should be easy to remember the changes to basic strategy when playing under these rules.

First, while standard basic strategy told you to split 2s and 3s against any dealer card from 2 through 7, you will not split as often if you cannot double after you split. You should not split 2s or 3s against a dealer showing a 2 or a 3. You will only split 2s or 3s against a dealer up card of 4 through 7. In all of these cases when you are not splitting, you should hit instead.

You also shouldn't split a pair of 6s against a 2. You will still split 6s against a dealer showing a 3 through 6. Against a 2, you should play the 6s as a 12, which means you should hit. (According to basic strategy, you hit 12 against 2.)

Finally, while the benchmark basic strategy told you to split 4s against a 5 or a 6, if you cannot double after you split, you should never split 4s. Instead, you should just hit the 8 against any dealer card.

The strategy chart for playing pairs when the player cannot double after splitting is provided below.

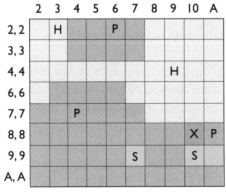

	2	3	4	5	6	7	8	9	10	A
2, 2		H			P					
3, 3										
4, 4							H			
6, 6										
7, 7			P							
8, 8									X	P
9, 9						S			S	
A, A										

Chart 23: Holding a pair, no doubling after split

To make it easier for you, the complete basic strategy when doubling is not allowed after splitting is provided at the end of the book, in Appendix D, on *page 113*.

SPANISH 21

As I discussed in Chapter 3, the alternative blackjack games such as Spanish 21 have different rules, and those different rules require a different playing strategy. If you were to attempt to play these games with the same basic strategy used for standard blackjack, you would lose at a much greater rate than usual. While it is beyond the scope of this book to provide a complete basic strategy for each of the alternative games I described, I will give a few examples of how the strategy differs. If you want to learn the best strategy for playing each of the games, you can find books that will provide complete basic strategies.

As you already learned, the main rule changes for Spanish 21 are the bonuses for certain combinations that form 21, the ability to double on any number of cards and then "rescue" the bet, and, most importantly, the use of a "Spanish deck" that doesn't include 10s. The greatly lowered chance of getting a 10-value card causes the most adjustments in the basic strategy. You should remember that our main assumption in our basic strategy came from the fact that you have a better chance of getting a 10 or face card than any other card. But, in Spanish 21, that chance is reduced by 25 percent due to the removal of the 10s from the deck. Because of this, we will be more wary of a dealer even with a seemingly bad up card of 5 or 6. (The chances are much lower that the dealer will have a 10 in the hole, making 15 or 16.) This "wariness" leads to the need to hit more hands, rather than standing and expecting the dealer to bust. Having fewer 10s in the deck reduces the dealer's chance of busting, but it also reduces the player's chance of busting. Therefore, in Spanish 21, the player should hit low hands like 12,

13, or 14 against low dealer up cards, including hands that the player would stand on in standard blackjack.

The number of 10-value cards in the deck affects the player's chances of hitting the right card when doubling. All of those 9s, 10s, and 11s that are perfect doubling opportunities in standard blackjack lead to many fewer 19s, 20s, and 21s in Spanish 21. Therefore, the basic strategy of Spanish 21 requires that the player double on fewer hands. While in regular blackjack, a player with a 10 or 11 should double against almost any dealer up card, in Spanish 21, the player will not double against the higher dealer cards, 9 through ace. With a hand equaling 9, the number of doubles decreases even more. The Spanish 21 player should only double with 9 against a dealer up card of 6, and hit against all other cards.

The bonuses in Spanish 21 affect basic strategy as well. When a player knows that he is well on his way to a possible bonus (if, for example, he has a 7♠ 7♠ or a 6♠ 8♠ and needs only another 7♠), he may want to take a hit to try to get the bonus when standing might actually provide a better chance of winning the hand. In addition, if the player has gotten three or four small cards to start his hand, he might have a chance at a bonus for a five- or six-card 21. Again, this would cause the player to take a hit to try to get to 21.

There are many examples of these cases. A player with two 7s would normally split them against a dealer showing a 7 himself. However, if those two 7s are the same suit, it is worth the chance at the bonus by taking a hit and hoping for a third suited 7, instead of splitting. There are many hands, such as 14s or 15s, that a player would not want to take a hit on, for fear of busting. But if the hands are made up of four or five cards already, and depending on the dealer's up card (the higher the dealer's card, the more cards the player should have to try this), the player should take a hit and try for the 21, rather than standing and hoping for the dealer to bust.

If re-doubling is allowed after doubling, the strategy gets even crazier. You might see a player doubling with just a hand of 5 or 6. It becomes worth the chance at getting another 4 or 5, and then being able to double again with 10 or 11. Of course, this is only done against a dealer with a very bad card showing, like a 6.

DOUBLE EXPOSURE BLACKJACK

Some of the basic strategy for playing Double Exposure Blackjack is obvious and couldn't be easier. For example, if you have a K♠ 8♥ and the dealer shows a 9♠ J♣, you know what you have to do: bite the bullet and take a hit, even though you have an 18. You know the dealer's final hand (19) and you know exactly what it takes to win. If you have 9♦ 9♣ and the dealer has K♠ 8♥, you should split. It is a better chance of winning than taking a hit on an 18, and you know you will lose if you stand. (Remember, ties go to the dealer in Double Exposure.)

It should be easy to figure out the strategy for dealer hands of 12 through 16. You already know what to do in standard blackjack when the dealer's up card is a 2 through 6, and we are only assuming that the hole card is a 10. Now we know for a fact that the dealer has a very bad hand. The strategy in these cases is to take even more advantage of the dealer's situation. In other words, the player should be more likely to double or split a hand (for example, doubling with a total of 8, or even 6 or 7, against a dealer showing 16).

But what happens when the dealer's first two cards only add up to something less than 12? In this case, we don't know the dealer's final total and we can't be sure what will happen. We must go back to our main assumption, that the next card out will have a value of 10. If we consider this, then we must treat hands of 10 or 11 as very dangerous hands (because the dealer is one card away from a 20 or 21) and hands of 5 or 6 as very advantageous hands for the player (because the dealer is one card away from the problematic 15 or 16). Much of the basic strategy for Double Exposure Blackjack follows these simple assumptions. The player should take advantage of a dealer showing a 5 or 6, and act warily towards a dealer showing a 10 or 11. For example, a player with a 4♥ 7♥ would normally double against a dealer showing a 6♠. In Double Exposure, the player should still double even the dealer's 6 is the total of both cards, say a 3♦ 3♠. Against a 5♦ 5♠, the same player should only hit.

The overall basic strategy for Double Exposure is generally easy to pick up, if you understand the basic strategy for standard blackjack. It is common sense, and of course, the more knowledge you have as a player, the safer your actions can be. However, there are more situations to worry about when you can see both of the dealer's cards, and there are subtle differences beyond what I've described above. If you choose to play Double Exposure, make sure you learn the strategy completely and not try to wing it at the table.

MULTIPLE-ACTION BLACKJACK

Here is some good news. The basic strategy for Multiple-Action Blackjack is the same as that for plain old single-action blackjack. The difference in the multi-action game is just the number of bets you make at one time. Because the dealer's up card will be the same for each of his three hands, and because you will only play your hand once, there is no difference in the actions you take or the information you have to base that action upon.

Remember that in Multiple-Action Blackjack, you can double one, two, or all three of your bets, and take insurance for one, two, or all three of your bets, but if you split, you must double all three bets. However, the strategy is simple in all three regards. As was the case for regular blackjack, if your hand is good enough to double and that is the correct strategy, it should be done to the maximum amount allowed. In other words, you should double all three bets exactly. You should never take insurance for even one of your bets, regardless of the cards you get. And your decision to split should be based on your pair and the dealer's up card, and not on your bet. If standard basic strategy says to split, then double all three bets and split your cards.

Multiple-Action Blackjack is one game you should not be afraid to play, if you know the basic strategy for blackjack. Of course, if you do not want to make three bets at a time and put three times as much money on every hand, then stick to classic blackjack.

SIDE BETS

The basic strategy for playing side bets is extremely easy: Do not play side bets!

As I showed in Chapter 3, the odds of side bets are made to be so far in the casino's favor that these are the biggest sucker bets in blackjack. I could tell you that it is a better bet to take the Over in an

Over/Under 13 side bet, but that should not imply that this is a good bet to make. It is still more than 5 percent in the casino's favor, which, when compared to standard blackjack's 0.5 to 1 percent casino edge, is a giant waste of your money. Other side bets are similar in their one-sidedness. Unless you are counting cards (and, in most cases, counting especially to find the best time to play the side bet), you should not play the side bets at all.

If you are a real gambler and can't pass up the action, if it is just too tempting to hit that big jackpot for three 7s of spades, then I suggest you find a blackjack table that does not offer any side bets.

REVIEW QUESTIONS

Here are a few more blackjack situations for you to practice basic strategy using different rule sets. For the first four questions, assume that the dealer hits on soft 17 (and all other rules are the same as the baseline in Chapter 3).

1. Player: 8♥ 8♦   Dealer: A♠
2. Player: 8♣ 9♠   Dealer: A♥
3. Player: Q♦ 5♦   Dealer: A♣
4. Player: 7♣ 4♥   Dealer: A♣

For the next four questions, assume that the dealer stands on all 17s, but doubling is not allowed after splitting (and all other rules are the same as the baseline in Chapter 2).

5. Player: 2♣ 2♦   Dealer: 4♥
6. Player: 3♦ 3♠   Dealer: 2♥
7. Player: 6♥ 6♣   Dealer: 2♠
8. Player: 4♥ 4♠   Dealer: 6♦

CHAPTER FIVE

COUNTING CARDS

You know the rules of blackjack and you know the basic strategy to use in any situation. You know enough to go into any casino and minimize the casino's edge down to less than one percent. But an edge of less than one percent is still an edge, and that means if you were to play this way you would still be a sucker—maybe the smartest sucker in the casino, but a sucker nonetheless.

To move the advantage to your favor instead of the casino's, you need to count cards. Counting cards in blackjack gives you the extra knowledge necessary to bet high when you are more likely to win and bet low when you are more likely to lose. Counting cards can also give you enough knowledge to make smarter playing decisions. You can fine-tune the strategy when you know the count, which makes you even more likely to win. In short, counting cards gives you the edge and makes you a winner.

CARD COUNTERS ARE NOT CRIMINALS (DESPITE WHAT THE CASINOS THINK)

Now is the time to dispel a few myths that you may have picked up while watching "Las Vegas Cheaters Exposed!!!" on the Travel Channel at three in the morning. These myths form the mystique of card counting. They are probably the biggest reason people dare not try counting cards themselves, despite the fact that it is easy to learn and can be managed by even the most risk-averse player.

MYTH #1:
CARD COUNTING IS NOT CHEATING

While casinos consider card counters as dangerous as cheaters to their bottom lines, it can hardly be considered cheating to play a game entirely within the rules, simply using one's intellect to outplay the average player. Is a chess grand champion considered a cheater for thinking 20 moves ahead of his adversary? The term "cheater" should really be reserved for people like the sleight-of-hand artist who can replace cards in his hand without the dealer or pit boss even noticing. Or the woman who places extra chips onto her bet *after* completing her hand and getting an unbeatable 21. Or the man who holds a tiny camera in the palm of his hand that spots the dealer's hole card and transmits the signal to a partner in the parking lot with sophisticated digital technology, who then signals a third teammate how to bet. These are all scams that have been used at blackjack tables around the world, and these are all against the rules of the game. Card counters don't use any devices or equipment, don't do anything to the cards or the chips, and don't gain any knowledge that every other player at the table doesn't also have. It simply cannot be called cheating.

MYTH #2:
CARD COUNTING IS ILLEGAL

The casinos want you to believe card counting is illegal, to deter you from trying it. The fact is that, even if a casino catches you counting cards, there is no law against it. They will never call the police, because there is nothing for the police to do. In fact, if you are caught counting cards, all the casino will do is ask you to stop playing blackjack. (Of course, they will also discontinue any comps they may have been giving you, but those are given at the casino's discretion, not by law.) Some casino personnel may treat you like a criminal if they believe you are counting cards, but that is merely intimidation (and frustration). It is as much a mental game as anything, in which the casino tries to make the card counter feel guilty for being good at the game, and uses that guilt to pressure a skilled blackjack player not to take advantage of his/her skill. Don't give in.

MYTH #3:
IF THEY CATCH YOU COUNTING CARDS, THEY MAY PHYSICALLY HURT YOU.

This is brought about by old stories and movies like *Casino*, in which the Mafia-run casinos take enforcement into their own hands. Perhaps in the past casino bosses would murder those they felt had mistreated or stolen from the casino and dispose of their bodies in a shallow grave out in the desert, but those days are long since gone. This is the twenty-first century, the age of giant hotel/casino conglomerates trading on the public stock markets. Casinos are monitored closely and security is professional and completely legal. These days, though a pit boss or casino manager may try to mentally intimidate you, no one will ever lay a hand on you. In fact, they will generally be very polite with you, even if they know you've been counting cards and have won thousands of dollars from them.

Having dispelled the myths, here is one important fact it is still best to remember.

Fact: Casinos know card counters can win, so if they know you are counting cards, they will bar you from playing blackjack.

You must always keep this in mind when playing blackjack in a casino. It is the reason you practice counting cards so much it becomes second nature. Amateurish mistakes like visibly counting numbers up on your hands or moving your lips as you count make you an obvious mark as a card counter. If you are betting large amounts, you are sure to attract the attention of casino personnel. It is absolutely necessary to come off looking like a normal gambler—a knowledgeable player, yes, but a gambler nonetheless. In addition, if you keep winning, or if your play is too obvious, pit bosses will start to suspect you. They will pay close attention, watching to see how you are playing. It's what the professionals call "heat." You must know when the heat is increasing and make your decision whether to continue playing and risk getting barred from playing, or "burned out."

However, if you are playing at lower limit tables and you are masking your play or just putting on a good facade, you should be able to play confidently without too much worry. I will give you some ideas for improving your chances of avoiding detection by the casino in later chapters. For now, just know that, no matter what the casinos and the TV shows say, you are not a bad person for counting cards, and go ahead and have fun while you do it.

IS COUNTING CARDS HARD TO DO?

When most people hear the term "card counter," they think of math geniuses with computers for brains. Or maybe they think of idiot savants, who can instantly count the number of toothpicks that fall from a box or do impossible long division in their heads. The biggest misconception is that counting cards means counting every card individually, and knowing exactly how many aces, 2s, 3s, etc., have been dealt from the deck (which, in the case of a six-deck shoe, could be up to 24 of each card).

The fact is that counting cards is easy. Just about anyone who can do simple arithmetic can count cards. It can be learned in minutes, and can be perfected with just some standard practice. If you can count from 1 to 10, then back down to 1 (then maybe down past zero to negative 10), you can count cards. The hardest math you will have to do will be to divide the count by the number of decks remaining, something like 5 divided by 4. And you don't need to be exact. You don't need to know 5 ÷ 4 = 1.25. It is enough to know that 5 divided by 4 is a little more than 1.

You will not need a photographic memory to count cards, either. You will not be memorizing every single card that passes by. All you will need to do is keep one number in your head, which will represent how many low cards and how many high cards have already been dealt. So don't be afraid. Keep reading this chapter and you will see how simple and powerful card counting is. And the only math you'll have to do is adding up all the money you win.

HOW DOES CARD COUNTING WORK?

How can something so simple reverse the big and powerful casino's edge in favor of the player? How can one number, "the count," represent enough knowledge that a player can change his bet and change his playing decisions to increase his chance of winning? The answer has already been provided in earlier chapters of this book. It is in the rules

of blackjack and the payouts, and it is in the basic strategy used to play your hand.

First, let's look at the rules of blackjack. What is the best hand to get, and also the way the player makes the most money? This is a "natural," or a blackjack. When the player is dealt an ace and a 10 or a face card, he wins one-and-a-half times his bet. Therefore, it follows that when there are more 10s, face cards, and especially aces left to be dealt, the player has a better chance of getting a blackjack, and therefore, a better chance of winning more money. Well, counting cards—knowing that one simple number—will tell you exactly when there are more 10s, face cards, and aces left in the deck(s).

Now, think back to the basic strategy you learned, and specifically, to the way it was formed. Our one big assumption was that the next card dealt would be a 10 or face card. That assumption drives many of the choices we make to play our hands. Basic strategy works because that assumption is based in statistical fact. When you count cards, you learn exactly when that assumption is most likely to be true. You will know when there are more 10s and face cards left to be dealt, and less of the low cards. The more often our basic assumption that the next card is a 10 is correct, the more often basic strategy works. That is why when you know the count, you will know when you are more likely to win.

Do the Math

In the last chapter, I showed you the numbers that revealed a player has a 42.32 percent chance of winning and a 57.68 percent chance of losing when standing with 14 against a dealer showing 6. But these odds were found assuming zero knowledge of past cards. In fact, I assumed these were the exact odds of each card coming up next that you would have when dealing from a newly shuffled deck.

When we count cards, we know when there are more 10s and aces, and fewer low cards. Does this really help us?

Let's re-run the numbers for a player with 14 against a 6, but let's change the odds a little. Now let's assume that, from a newly shuffled complete deck, we take one 2, one 3, one 4, and one 5, and we add in four 10s (or face cards, it doesn't matter) in their place. What does this do to the odds of receiving any one card value? The chart below shows the old and new odds:

CARD	OLD NUMBER IN DECK	OLD ODDS	NEW NUMBER IN DECK	NEW ODDS
Ace	4	7.69%	4	7.69%
Two	4	7.69%	3	5.77%
Three	4	7.69%	3	5.77%
Four	4	7.69%	3	5.77%
Five	4	7.69%	3	5.77%
Six	4	7.69%	4	7.69%
Seven	4	7.69%	4	7.69%
Eight	4	7.69%	4	7.69%
Nine	4	7.69%	4	7.69%
Ten (or Face)	16	30.77%	20	38.46%

Chart 24. Odds of Receiving Any One Card Value with One 2, 3, 4, 5 Removed from Newly Shuffled Deck and Four 10s Added

As you can see, there is now more than a 38 percent chance of getting a 10 (our main assumption) versus just over 30 percent before.

Now, let's see what these new odds do to the dealer's chances of busting. Of course, the dealer is showing a 6 so, right away, we can see that there is an increased chance the dealer's two-card hand will be a 16. In fact, the new odds for the dealer's hole card are exactly the new odds shown above. That means there is an almost 8 percent greater chance that the dealer will have a 16 with two cards.

Given the new probabilities of each card being dealt, we can recalculate the probabilities of the dealer's final hand. Starting with 16, we repeat the process we used before. The odds of the final dealer hand, given a two-card hand of 16, can be found using the new odds for the third card dealt:

17 (Ace [1] + 16)	4-out-of-52	7.69%
18 (2 + 16)	3-out-of-52	5.77%
19 (3 + 16)	3-out-of-52	5.77%
20 (4 + 16)	3-out-of-52	5.77%
21 (5 + 16)	3-out-of-52	5.77%
22 (6 + 16)	4-out-of-52	7.69%
23 (7 + 16)	4-out-of-52	7.69%
24 (8 + 16)	4-out-of-52	7.69%
25 (9 + 16)	4-out-of-52	7.69%
26 (10 + 16)	20-out-of-52	38.46%

Therefore, by adding up the busting hands (22 through 26), the odds of the dealer getting each final hand when he starts with a 16 are the following:

17	7.69%
18	5.77%
19	5.77%
20	5.77%
21	5.77%
BUST	69.23%

Compare that to the odds with a standard deck of cards:

17	7.69%
18	7.69%
19	7.69%
20	7.69%
21	7.69%
BUST	61.54%

Clearly, with the extra 10s in the deck, the dealer has a greater chance of busting, and when he doesn't bust, he is more likely to end up with 17 than with anything higher.

Continuing the calculations with two-card hands of 15, our new three-card total probabilities are:

16 (Ace [I] + 15)	4-out-of-52	7.69%
17 (2 + 15)	3-out-of-52	5.77%
18 (3 + 15)	3-out-of-52	5.77%
19 (4 + 15)	3-out-of-52	5.77%
20 (5 + 15)	3-out-of-52	5.77%
21 (6 + 15)	4-out-of-52	7.69%
22 (7 + 15)	4-out-of-52	7.69%
23 (8 + 15)	4-out-of-52	7.69%
24 (9 + 15)	4-out-of-52	7.69%
25 (10 + 15)	20-out-of-52	38.46%

In the case that the third card is an ace, the dealer will take another card. Again, we calculate the odds by multiplying the 7.69 percent chance that the third card is an ace by the odds of each final hand (after dealing a fourth card), which are the odds we just found for a two-card hand of 16. Adding those odds to the third-card odds above, we get the following final hand probabilities:

17	5.77% + 0.59% = 6.36%
18	5.77% + 0.44% = 6.21%
19	5.77% + 0.44% = 6.21%
20	5.77% + 0.44% = 6.21%
21	7.69% + 0.44% = 8.14%
BUST	61.54% + 5.33% = 66.87%

The calculations follow for every two-card possibility in the same way as before, though in this case, we will see that the odds of busting will be higher due to the extra 10s, until we get to two-card hands of

8 through 11. Let's take 11, for example. If the dealer flips over the hole card to reveal a 5, he has 11 and must take another card. The odds of three-card hands will be:

12 (Ace [I] + 11)	4-out-of-52	7.69%
13 (2 + 11)	3-out-of-52	5.77%
14 (3 + 11)	3-out-of-52	5.77%
15 (4 + 11)	3-out-of-52	5.77%
16 (5 + 11)	3-out-of-52	5.77%
17 (6 + 11)	4-out-of-52	7.69%
18 (7 + 11)	4-out-of-52	7.69%
19 (8 + 11)	4-out-of-52	7.69%
20 (9 + 11)	4-out-of-52	7.69%
21 (10 + 11)	20-out-of-52	38.46%

In this case, the hand that will hurt us the most, the 21, will come up the most often. In addition, there is no way for the dealer to bust except for the hands that will require dealing more cards, but those hands (12 through 16) are less likely to happen, due to the reduction in 2s through 5s. In this case, the new odds hurt us. The final hand odds for a dealer whose first two cards make 11 are:

17	9.88%
18	9.88%
19	10.00%
20	10.13%
21	41.04%
BUST	19.07%

Compare this to the probabilities given a standard deck of cards:

17	11.14%
18	11.14%
19	11.14%
20	11.14%
21	34.22%
BUST	21.21%

Dealer ends up with: →	17	18	19	20	21	BUST
Dealer's first two cards						
8	11.27%	41.96%	11.33%	5.59%	5.78%	24.07%
9	10.57%	10.50%	41.40%	10.76%	5.02%	21.74%
10	9.88%	9.81%	9.93%	40.83%	10.19%	19.35%
11	9.88%	9.88%	10.00%	10.13%	41.04%	19.07%
12	7.51%	9.30%	9.45%	9.57%	9.70%	54.47%
13	7.10%	6.97%	8.89%	9.04%	9.16%	58.85%
14	6.70%	6.58%	6.58%	8.50%	8.65%	62.98%
15	6.36%	6.21%	6.21%	6.21%	8.14%	66.86%
16	7.69%	5.77%	5.77%	5.77%	5.77%	69.23%

Chart 25

Dealer ends up with: →	17	18	19	20	21	BUST
Dealer's Hole card						
2	0.65%	2.42%	0.65%	0.32%	0.33%	1.39%
3	0.61%	0.61%	2.39%	0.62%	0.29%	1.25%
4	0.57%	0.57%	0.57%	2.36%	0.59%	1.12%
5	0.57%	0.57%	0.58%	0.58%	2.37%	1.10%
6	0.58%	0.72%	0.73%	0.74%	0.75%	4.19%
7	0.55%	0.54%	0.68%	0.70%	0.70%	4.53%
8	0.52%	0.51%	0.51%	0.65%	0.67%	4.84%
9	0.49%	0.48%	0.48%	0.48%	0.63%	5.14%
10, Jack, Queen or King	2.96%	2.22%	2.22%	2.22%	2.22%	26.63%
Ace	7.69%	0.00%	0.00%	0.00%	0.00%	0.00%

Chart 26

Clearly, the new odds hurt us in this case. There is a lower chance of busting and a higher chance of the dealer's getting a 21, which we cannot possibly beat. However, the good news is that the dealer can only make a two-card hand of eleven 5.77 percent of the time, rather than 7.69 percent of the time with a standard deck.

Creating a chart of all of the percentages for every final hand and every two-card starting hand, we get Chart 25, *above*.

Once again, we take the probabilities that any of those two-card hands will actually come up and multiply those by the final-hand percentages to get the percentages that any of these situations will occur as shown in Chart 26, *above*.

By adding up all of the rows for each column, we can find the correct odds for the dealer finishing with any hand. The final odds of each hand, given the adjusted deck, are:

17	15.18%
18	8.62%
19	8.81%
20	8.67%
21	8.54%
BUST	50.19%

Now, we can compare the difference the extra 10s made on the final odds. Here are the odds given a standard deck:

17	16.54%
18	10.63%
19	10.63%
20	10.17%
21	9.72%
BUST	42.32%

Just as before, we have stood with a 14 and let the dealer hit, so the only way we can win is for the dealer to bust, and any time the dealer makes a hand of 17 through 21 we will lose. But now, the dealer will bust 50.19 percent of the time and will make a hand only 49.81% of the time. This means we win 50.19 percent of the time, or 7.87 percent more often than when the card is coming from a newly shuffled full deck. With only four small cards taken away and four 10s added, we will win an extra $7.87 for every $100 bet, and we will even have the edge when we get a 14 and the dealer has a 6 showing.

Let's look again at the possible play of hitting the 14 against the dealer's 6. Looking at the chart above of final-hand odds given a two-card starting hand of 14, we get the following odds:

17	6.70%
18	6.58%
19	6.58%
20	8.50%
21	8.65%
BUST	62.98%

We can already see that, since we bust 62.98 percent of the time, we are much

worse off taking a hit. But let's complete the calculations. Again, we can build a chart of our chances of winning, tying, or losing, based on the dealer's odds of any given hand, as shown in Chart 27, on *the following page*.

Now, we multiply those percentages by the percentage chance that we will actually finish with any of those hands. This gives us the following odds, as shown in Chart 28, on *the following page*.

By adding the columns up for each row, we get our final odds of winning or losing:

You Win	27.50%
You Push or Tie	3.64%
You Lose	68.88%

If you were to hit your 14 with the adjusted deck, you would lose $41.38 for every $100 bet. Compare that to the $34.00 you would lose when hitting your 14 with a standard deck, or to the $0.38 you would win if you stand with 14, and you see how important it is, even with the count high, to stick to the correct strategy.

That is one example of how the player's advantage grows when there are more 10s left to be dealt. In fact, the player's advantage will grow right in line with the relative number of high cards to low cards left. That is why counting only this one number gives us enough knowledge to make betting and playing decisions.

It is easy to see that, if counting cards tells us when we are more likely to win, then we can use it to determine when to bet higher. If you were forced to make two different bets and you were told you would win one bet 25 percent of the time

When you get:	17	18	19	20	21	BUST
You win	50.19%	65.37%	73.99%	82.79%	91.46%	0.00%
You tie	15.18%	8.62%	8.81%	8.67%	8.54%	0.00%
You lose	34.63%	26.01%	17.21%	8.54%	0.00%	100.00%

Chart 27

When you get:	17	18	19	20	21	BUST
You win	3.38%	4.30%	4.87%	7.04%	7.91%	0.00%
You tie	1.02%	0.57%	0.58%	0.74%	0.74%	0.00%
You lose	2.33%	1.71%	1.13%	0.73%	0.00%	62.98%

Chart 28

and the other 75 percent of the time, you wouldn't have to think long to know you wanted to bet more on the second bet. That is exactly how card-counting works. You will bet more when the count is high, meaning there are more 10s and aces in the deck or shoe, relative to the small cards, which happens to also be the time you are more likely to win. And you will either bet low, or not bet at all, when the count is low, meaning you are less likely to win.

HOW TO COUNT CARDS

There are several different systems for counting cards. All of them have the same goal: to know when there are more 10s and aces left relative to the small cards. The differences between the systems are in the details of how you count each card. Some are more complex, giving different values to each card, requiring you to not only see the cards but know the value associated with that card and add that to your count.

The system that I will teach in this book is very simple. It is called the "high-low" count, because you simply subtract or add one to the count for each high or low card. It is extremely easy to learn and, with practice, it becomes an almost unconscious process, allowing you to use important mental energy on things like making playing decisions or talking to the pit boss who's hanging around your table. It is true that a more complex counting system can give you a little more knowledge about the cards left in the shoe, but experience shows that the extra edge you get from the increased knowledge is offset by the difficulty of counting. With a complex system, it's very possible a counting error will take away all of the edge you gain by playing that complex system. I will discuss a couple more complex counting systems at the end of this chapter, if you've mastered the high-low count and you're looking for a challenge.

Here is how to count using the high-low system: When you see a high card, subtract one; when you see a low card, add one. It is exactly that easy. All you need to know is which cards are "high" and which are "low." Chart 29, on *page 70*, tells you how to count each card:

CARD	HIGH OR LOW	HOW TO COUNT
Two	Low	+1
Three	Low	+1
Four	Low	+1
Five	Low	+1
Six	Low	+1
Seven	–	0
Eight	–	0
Nine	–	0
Ten	High	–1
Jack	High	–1
Queen	High	–1
King	High	–1
Ace	High	–1

Chart 29. How to Count Using the High-Low System

When the dealer shuffles, or when you first come to a table, you will start the count at 0. As the dealer deals each card, you will either add or subtract from the count according to the chart above. For example, the dealer shuffles and gets ready to start. Your count is 0. The dealer deals you two cards: 4♥ J♣. When you see the 4♥, you add 1, making the count 1. When you see the J♣, you subtract 1, making the count 0 again. That is all there is to it. Just continue to add and subtract for every card (except, of course, for sevens, eights and nines, which are neutral cards.) In this way, you will always have a running count of the number of low cards that have already been dealt relative to the number of high cards that have been dealt. This is called the "relative count."

Here are a couple more examples:

Example 1. The cards come out as follows: 3♠ A♠ 7♥ 10♣ 2♦ 7♣ 3♠ Q♥. The relative count is now 0. For every high card that came out, there was also a low card. The count goes like this: 1, 0, 0, –1, 0, 0, 1, 0.

Example 2. You have been counting a shoe and the relative count currently stands at 9. The next cards out are: A♥ 10♠ K♣ K♥ J♦ 10♥ Q♠ A♥ 10♦. The relative count is now 0. Every card was a high card, and so you would subtract 1 for each card. The count goes from 9 to this: 8, 7, 6, 5, 4, 3, 2, 1, 0.

Practice Makes Perfect

While learning basic strategy requires rote memorization and serious study, learning to count (fast) requires nothing more than practice, practice, practice. You must practice counting over and over, and also faster and faster, until you can count quickly and precisely without even thinking about it.

There is a very easy way to practice counting, and all it requires is a deck of cards. Take the deck and turn it face up. Now simply riffle through the cards, one at a time, keeping the relative count as you go. Because there are an equal number of high cards and low cards in a deck, when you get to the end, your count should equal zero. This is a good check that you have counted correctly. (Make sure you have a complete deck before you start, or you could get very frustrated very fast.) In the beginning, you may want to say the count aloud after each card you see. But as you get better, you should switch to keeping the count in your head, because that is what you will have to do in a casino.

Practicing with this method is very useful, because you can vary the speed yourself. Start out going slow, making sure that you get the count right. At first, you will have to think about which card you are looking at and whether you should be adding or subtracting one. With practice, that will become more automatic and you will

AT THE TABLE

Here is a tip to make counting the cards easier: Count cards two at a time.

Because an equal number of cards count for +1 and −1, you will find that many times a pair of cards balance out to 0 and you don't even have to worry about them. Look again at Example 1 above. The cards were 3♠ A♠ 7♥ 10♣ 2♦ 7♣ 3♠ Q♥. Now take them in pairs: (3♠ A♠) (7♥ 10♣) (2♦ 7♣) (3♠ Q♥). In terms of counting, the pairs equal (+1 −1) (0 −1) (+1 0) (+1 −1). You can see that the first and the last pair balance out to 0. Thus, counting in pairs, you would have 0, −1, +1, 0, which adds up to 0.

You will find if you practice counting in pairs that you will quickly see a zero-pair, such as (3♠ A♠) or (3♠ Q♥), and know right away to ignore it. In addition, because players' hands are dealt in pairs, you will find this is a faster and more efficient way to count a table full of cards that have already been dealt.

be able to speed up your deal. Do not go faster than you can accurately count. The key is to keep an error-free count in your head. If you are making errors in counting, it doesn't matter how fast you can go. As you speed up, you will get to the point where you can count cards faster than they would ever be dealt in a casino—although you will be surprised sometimes how fast a dealer can deal when you are the only one at the table.

You should also practice counting the cards in pairs. You can use the same method to practice pairs. Just look at two cards at a time. Learn to see neutral pairs (i.e., a high card paired with a low card) quickly and move on to the next pair. This, too, will become automatic for you if you practice it enough.

When you're feeling confident in your counting and you want an extra challenge, try this. Take a couple decks of cards together. As long as you use complete decks, the final count should still come to zero. Now, go through the decks and pull out some of the low cards (or some of the high cards). Then shuffle them into a

small section at the beginning or the end of the pile. This will make the count go up or down more than it would naturally, which makes it more difficult to count (because the numbers will be different from what you are used to, and because there will be fewer neutral pairs if that is how you are counting).

When you think you're an expert at counting, and you never lose track of the count or make a mistake, you should start to add in some distractions. The casino environment is full of distractions. There are other people at the table, talking to each other and to you. There are other games going on all around you. You may be near a TV or live music or some other entertainment. And, most distracting of all, you will hear numbers being spoken all the time. Many dealers will add up players' hands and say the totals out loud. Some players will call out the number of the card they want from the dealer. Sometimes, a player will cash in or out and the dealer will call out the amount of money. You will be bombarded with numbers, but it is imperative you be able to filter those numbers out and keep a hold of the one number that matters to you—the count.

So practice with distractions. Turn the television on while you practice counting. Talk to a friend, roommate, or spouse. You may even want someone to yell out numbers while you count. Practice this way and you will get expert at filtering out distractions, counting cards, and remembering the count.

It is not advised to practice counting at the casino. While it is good to get used to counting in the environment in which you will be playing, you have no way of knowing what the actual count is at any time. Because the dealer always shuffles before he gets to the end of the shoe and you never know what cards are left unseen when the shuffle happens, the count will not always end at zero. And that means that you will never know whether your count is correct, so you will never know when you have mastered counting the cards.

If you want to practice counting cards and playing blackjack at the same time, I suggest using a computer blackjack game. Most blackjack software will keep the count for you and can be set to show or not show the count as it changes. You will be able to play blackjack, watch the cards that come up, and keep your own count, then double-check your count against what the computer says it is. Some blackjack games will let you set the speed of the dealer, so you can start slow and work your way up to speed. Practice playing head up (one on one) with the dealer, and with varying numbers of other (virtual) players, so you get a feel for counting other players' hands.

THE "TRUE COUNT"

Now you know how to count the cards and maintain a running "relative count" of low cards versus high cards. Since you are adding one when you see a low card and subtracting one when you see a high card, the higher the number, the more low cards you have seen and/or the fewer high cards you have seen. That means that the number of low cards you have seen relative to the number of high cards you have seen is high when the count is high. That tells us that, in the cards still remaining to be seen, there are fewer low cards than 10s and aces. In other words, when the relative count is high, there are more high cards left in the shoe than there are low cards. And that is exactly what we want.

So the higher the relative count, the better. Well, not exactly. The relative count tells us how many high cards are left in the shoe, relative to small cards. But it provides us with incomplete information. Let's take an example. Say the relative count is +6. That means six more low cards than high cards have been dealt already. It could be that six low cards and no high cards have come out, or it could be that 20 low cards have come out and 14 high cards have been dealt. In either case, we know that there are six more high cards than low cards left in the shoe.

But the information that we don't know from the relative count is just how many total cards are left in the shoe. This is very important, because it determines how advantageous the difference in high cards versus low cards is at any time. In our example, we know that there are six more high cards than low cards left in the shoe. But what we really need to know is what the chances are that the next card to come out will be one of those high cards. There may be six more high cards than low cards, but if there are still many cards left to be seen, the difference of six means much less than if there were only a few cards left. (If there were only six cards left to be dealt, we would know that all of those cards would be 10s or aces.)

Do the Math

Let's look at this example in terms of odds of getting a 10 or an ace. Let's assume a six-deck shoe. Before the shuffle, we know the odds of getting a 10 or ace are 96-in-312 (or 4 suits × 4 different cards × 6 decks out of 52 cards × 6 decks), which equals 30.8 percent. (Of course, it's the same as the odds for only one deck.)

Now, if the first six cards to come out are low cards, we know that there are six more high cards than low cards left in the 306 (312 − 6) cards remaining. So now the odds of catching a 10 or ace are 96-in-306, or 31.4 percent. A little better, but not much different.

But, if there are only two decks worth of cards remaining and we still know that there are six more high cards than low cards among those two decks, what are the odds? We have 104 cards remaining. Let's assume an average number of neutral cards (7s, 8s, and 9s) came out, which means there will be 24 of those cards remaining (24 = 3 cards × 4 suits × 2 decks). Since there are six more high cards than low cards in the other 80 cards, we have 43 high cards and 37 low cards left. So, now the chance that the next card will be a 10 or an ace is 43-in-104, or 41.3 percent.

The difference between a relative count of 6 with almost six full decks left and a relative count of 6 with only two decks left is almost exactly 10 percentage points. That is why a higher relative count is not always better. A count of 10 early on in a shoe may not be as valuable as a count of 5 late in the shoe.

In order to make the relative count into a number that more accurately reflects our actual chances of winning, we have to take into account the number of cards that are remaining to be played. This is done by dividing the relative count by the number of decks remaining to be played. This simple calculation creates one number that represents the number of excess high cards in each deck remaining in the shoe, and this number can be used to make decisions no matter where in the shoe play falls. This number is called the "true count." When a card counter wants to know how many high cards remain relative to the low cards, he will ask "what is the count?" But when he wants to know how many excess high cards remain per deck, he will instead ask "what is the true?" (Of course, anyone can show up at a table and, hearing the relative count, can figure out the true count for himself, so a counter will not usually ask for the true count.)

Let's look at a couple more examples:

Example 1. The relative count is 6 and there are two decks remaining in the shoe. Divide the relative count by the number of decks remaining to get the true count. In this case, the true count is 6 ÷ 2, or 3.

Example 2. It doesn't always work out so cleanly. What if the relative count is 6 and there are four decks remaining? In this case, the true count is 6 ÷ 4, or 1½. Do not round the number. Just remember the true count as 1½. If, on the other hand, there were five decks remaining, the true count would be 6 ÷ 5, or 1.2. In that case, you don't really need to be so exact. You might think of it as almost one and a quarter, or as a little more than one.

Example 3. The relative count can also

AT THE TABLE

To turn the relative count into the true count, you need to know how many decks are remaining to be dealt. This is easier than it sounds. You do not need to know the exact number, but the closer you can get to the correct number, the closer your bet will be to optimal. Of course, you could actually count how many cards get dealt, to know the exact number. But I would be very impressed by the person who could know the relative count of low cards to high cards dealt was 7, and the number of cards that had been dealt was 113, leaving 199 remaining in a six-deck shoe, and that his cards added up to 19 while the dealer just got a 7 to bust her hand at 23. Oh yeah, and know all that while talking to the pit boss who just strolled by talking about last night's exciting 24-13 football game. It's just asking too much of your mind.

Instead, you will simply estimate the number of decks remaining. Luckily for the card counter, the casinos, in order to show that they do not cheat, keep the cards in view of the players at all times. That means that before any cards are dealt, you can see the full six (or two, or eight) decks in front of you. It also means that, as the cards get played, they are discarded into a pile, which is also left on the table in view of the players. So you will also always see the cards that have already been dealt. Once they have been shuffled, the cards are placed into a plastic container called a shoe. The shoe is made so it is easy for the dealer to remove one card at a time, without revealing any of the cards to the players. Because of the way the cards sit in the shoe, and the shoe being made of colored plastic in most cases, it is difficult to see exactly how many cards are in the shoe. So it is difficult to estimate from looking at the shoe how many decks are left to be dealt.

It is easier to look at the pile of cards that have already been played and estimate from that how many decks are still left in the shoe. The discards are placed neatly in a pile, standing up vertically rather than laid down horizontally as in the shoe, inside a clear plastic container to the dealer's right. That makes it much easier to see the discards than the cards that are still remaining to be dealt. The discard pile is placed to the dealer's right, just next to the player at third base. If you are sitting at third base, you may find it difficult to see the pile as well, or to look at the discards without being obvious about it. Play different positions to see what feels most comfortable to you. Obviously, all of the cards in the discard pile plus all of the cards on the table plus all of the cards in the shoe will add up to the full six decks being played. Therefore, you will simply estimate how many decks have already been played (from looking at the discard pile) and subtract that from the six deck's total.

The only thing you need to be able to do is to estimate by looking at a pile of cards how many decks are in that pile. You do not need to be perfect, but try to be as exact as you can. Especially when the numbers are low, a small error can make a real difference in the way you bet. For example, let's say the relative count is 6. If you look at the discard pile and estimate that three out of six decks have been played, that leaves three remaining and your true count will be 2 ($6 \div 3 = 2$). But if you look at the same pile and estimate that it equals four decks worth of cards, then you will think there are two remaining and your true count will be 3 ($6 \div 2 = 3$). This will make a big difference in the way you bet on your next hand.

So you should practice estimating the number of decks in a pile. Get yourself six decks of cards and put cards together in piles of one deck, two decks, one-and-a-half decks, etc. Get a good eye for how many decks in a pile. It can only help you make a better estimate of the true count and, therefore, a smarter bet. Any error you make reduces your edge over the casino, so don't get too sloppy when calculating your true count.

There are going to be times when you may miss seeing a card or two, or even an entire deck's worth of cards. For example, you may walk over to a table where the cards have just been shuffled, but you are a little too late to see the first couple rounds of hands. In those cases, you don't necessarily have to give up on the entire shoe. However, you do need to account for the unseen cards. The way to do that is to simply add the cards you missed to the number of cards remaining to be dealt. (In fact, to be exact, this is the number of cards you haven't seen, not the number you are yet to see.) So, if you get to a table and there is half a deck's worth of cards in the discard pile, just remember to always add ½ a deck to the remaining cards before you calculate the true count. That way, you are still diluting the value of the relative number of high cards by the correct amount. Of course, if you have missed a half a shoe, you probably want to find another table, because you lose your edge with all those cards you will never see. (You will always be dividing your relative count by at least 3, so your true count probably won't get very high.)

be negative, and so can the true count. If the relative count is −4 and there are two decks remaining, then the true count will be −4 ÷ 2, or −2. Do not lose track of the negative.

OTHER COUNTING METHODS

Math geniuses have invented several different methods for counting cards, hoping to increase their edge over the casino. The high-low count is generally the preferred counting system, because it gives the player enough information to gain a real advantage, but it is simple enough to maintain in the heat of the high-rolling battle. However, there are several other counting systems that players use to gain an edge.

For example, there is a counting system called the "halves" count. This counting system actually provides more information on the cards left to be dealt, because it is more detailed than the simple high-low count. The halves count is called that because it gives card values estimated to the half, rather than just 1 or 0. In the halves count, cards that are dealt are counted as follows:

CARD	HOW TO COUNT
Two	+ 0.5
Three	+ 1
Four	+ 1
Five	+ 1.5
Six	+ 1
Seven	+ 0.5
Eight	0
Nine	− 0.5
Ten	− 1
Jack	− 1
Queen	− 1
King	− 1
Ace	− 1

Chart 30. How to count halves

As you can see, this counting system is much more detailed and, therefore, much more difficult to utilize without making errors. The differences are in the fact that the 2 is a less dangerous card for the player, because it is less likely to break the player's hand, while the 5 is more dangerous for the opposite reason. This is reflected in the lower value of the 2s and the higher value of the 5s. In addition, the cards 7 and 9 are given values, rather than the 0 they are worth in the simpler counting system.

This system, like the high-low count, is a balanced count, meaning an entire deck of cards will still add up to zero. You can effectively use the same strategies for betting and for playing your hands with the halves count as you use for the high-low count. And because you have more information included in your count, you will actually win more money if you can successfully keep the count. You will also find that your "luck" is not as important using the halves count, because it more often correctly predicts the cards left in the shoe. (That means you will have smaller swings of winning and losing.)

If you think you can keep the halves count and want to try, just remember a couple of things. Even if you count perfectly, the difference over the high-low system will only be a few per hour. But just a few small errors in counting can completely wipe out that edge and then some. That is why the professionals generally stick with the simple but powerful high-low count.

But there are other counts, as well. There is also a count called the "Hi-Opt" count. The Hi-Opt count is very similar to the high-low count. Cards are all equal to either 1 or 0 and the total of all cards in the deck will still add up to 0. The difference is that the Hi-Opt count ignores the 2s and aces. Twos are equal to 0, rather than plus 1. Aces are equal to 0, rather than −1. We have seen, from the halves count, that 2s should be valued lower than they are in the high-low count, but why ignore aces?

Counting systems are used for two separate uses: to determine how much to bet, and to determine how to play your hand. It turns out that aces and 10s are definitely not equal in value when determining how to play one's hand. Remember that our basic strategy generally relies on the greater chance of the player catching a 10 or the dealer busting with a 10. An ace does not always help the same amount. For example, imagine standing with 12 because the dealer has a 6 showing only to find that the dealer has an ace in the hole, for a 17 (not the 16 you were hoping for).

So you may actually be hurting your strategy for playing your hand by counting aces as −1 in the count. However, you may also remember that blackjacks are worth 50 percent more than regular wins, and you can't have a blackjack without an ace. Therefore, knowing when you have a better chance of getting an ace is very valuable. The Hi-Opt count may help you make better decisions at playing your hand, but it doesn't help you bet more when you have a better chance of getting a blackjack, which is actually much more valuable to you in the long run.

Some people propose counting using the Hi-Opt count and, at the same time, keeping a running count of only aces. That way, you could use the first count for playing strategy and also the second count for betting strategy. The drawback of this system is pretty obvious. You go ahead and try to keep two counts in your head.

There are other counts, as well. There are counts like the halves count, but that double the index numbers so that you needn't remember halves. Of course, you would have to double the numbers you use for strategies. There are also some unbalanced counts that include the 7 in the count, but not the 8 or 9. The "KO" count is the same as the high-low, but the 7 counts as +1, while the "Red 7" counts only sevens of hearts or diamonds as +1.

You can find many different counting systems in various books and sites on the Internet. All of them work to some extent, and you should simply use what you feel most confident with. And make sure you practice, no matter what you choose.

REVIEW QUESTIONS

Time for a little counting practice. For the first five questions, assume the cards listed are the cards that get dealt at a blackjack table. Keep the count as you would if you were at the table. The answers, on *pages 121 and 122* will show the running count, as well as the final count you should have calculated.

1. A♦ 10♣ 9♦ 2♥ 2♦ 5♠ 6♦ 7♥ 4♣ 4♥ Q♦ 5♥
2. 6♦ 8♠ Q♠ 7♠ 8♦ A♦ K♦ J♥ A♣ 6♠ 6♣ 7♥
3. 2♦ 5♦ 4♣ 10♦ 7♣ J♣ K♣ 8♣ A♦ 6♣ J♠ 8♦
4. A♦ 4♣ Q♦ Q♣ K♦ 6♥ 5♦ 7♠ 8♥ 7♣ 4♥ 3♠
5. 7♦ 5♣ 9♠ A♣ J♦ 7♣ 7♠ 10♣ 3♦ 2♥ 5♦ Q♣

For the next three questions, you should calculate the true count based on the information you're given. Try to be as exact as you can.

6. The relative count is 12. There are three decks remaining in the shoe. What is the true count?
7. The relative count is 10. You are playing in an eight-deck blackjack game and four decks have been dealt. What is the true count?
8. The relative count is 12. You didn't sit down until half a deck had already been dealt and there are now only two decks left in the shoe. What is the true count?

CHAPTER SIX

BETTING TO WIN

So far, you have learned basic strategy, so you know how to play every hand, and you have also learned how to count cards, which tells you when you are likeliest to win. All that you need to know now is how much to bet and when to bet it. That is the final piece of the puzzle. After reading this chapter, you will be able to go to a casino and, betting optimally according to an accurate count, you will be able to win money.

BETTING ACCORDING TO THE COUNT

I have already told you that what counting cards does for you is tell you when you are most likely to win. You win in blackjack not by winning more hands than you lose. You win by betting more money when you win than you do when you lose. Because you know the count, you know when you are more likely to win, which, in turn, tells you when you should bet higher.

In simple terms, the rule is this: Bet high when the count is high. The converse is true, as well. You should bet low (or even better, don't bet at all) when the count is low. For some people, this is all they will do to bet. They might pick a bet amount for a low count and a higher bet amount for a high count. (*Note:* the "count" that you will use to calculate your bet should always be the true count, not the relative count. The true count represents your actual chances of winning, because it factors in the number of cards

left. Therefore, a true count of 3 means the same thing whether there are two decks left or four decks left.) For example, a very simple betting system would be to bet $10 when the true count is below 2, and bet $25 when the true count is 2 or higher. Clearly, this would mean a higher bet when you are more likely to win (because a count of 2 or higher does mean a better chance of winning). Using this system, you would win more (in the long run) than if you just bet $10 or $25 on every hand, regardless of the count. But this system would not take full advantage of the count. Because the count goes up and down in direct relation to your chance of winning, an optimal betting strategy will take into account how high the count is.

A more advantageous betting strategy will allow the bets the flexibility to grow with the count, so that a very high count will equal more value than a somewhat high count. This is done by using the true count as a sort of multiplier, to calculate your optimal bet. The basic method will be to take a number and multiply it by the true count (with some adjustments) to come up with the amount that you should bet. But what number will you multiply to get your bet? That is something called the "unit bet." Your unit bet is the amount that you base your bet calculations upon, but it does not necessarily mean that you will frequently (or ever) bet exactly the unit bet. It is simply a baseline.

You should decide before you start playing what your unit bet will be. This number is based on how much money you have and how much you want to play (which is probably determined by how much you want to win, or perhaps how much you can afford to lose). A beginning card counter may start with a $5 unit bet when first practicing at a casino. Someone who is very risk-averse and just wants to play blackjack for fun and not risk losing much money would also want to play a small unit. (Counting cards gives you the edge, which translates to winning in the long run, but it doesn't protect you from losing streaks or bad luck in the short term.) Meanwhile, it would not be a stretch for a professional card counter to play a $1,000 or $2,000 unit bet. The betting strategy works the same, whether you play a $10, $100, or $1,000 unit bet.

To determine how much you should bet, first take the true count and subtract a number that represents the house's advantage for the particular table you are playing. This number changes, because the rules change. In one casino, you may be able to surrender and the dealer may stand on soft 17s, while in another casino, surrender may not be allowed and dealers may hit soft 17s. Sometimes you will even find different rules at different tables in the same casino. Because some rules give the casino a greater advantage over you than others, you need to take these rules into account before you bet. If you are playing at a table with disadvantageous rules, you will need to have a higher count to gain an edge over the casino. That means you want the count to be higher

before you start betting higher. That is why you subtract this "casino advantage factor" from the true count.

I will use the following rule set as a baseline for determining what number to subtract from the true count: Surrender available, dealer stands on soft 17s, doubling allowed after splits, split to four hands, and no re-splitting of aces. Given this set of rules, which are not egregiously in favor of the house, the casino's advantage just after a shuffle (or any time the count is exactly 0) is about .25 percent. A true count of 1 represents an increased advantage of about .5 percent. (That means, every 1 you add to the true count is an extra .5 percent in your favor. Similarly, every 1 the true count goes down represents a gain of .5 percent edge for the casino.) Because .25 percent is half of .5 percent, the casino's edge at the beginning of the shoe is equal to ½ in true count terms. Therefore, your casino advantage factor will be ½. When playing the benchmark rules, subtract ½ from the true count to get your bet multiplier. Then, multiply that number by your unit bet. The number you come up with is the amount you should bet.

Example 1. Your relative count is 9. (You have seen nine more low cards than 10s and aces.) There are two decks remaining in the shoe, so your true count is 4½ (9 ÷ 2 = 4½). You are playing by the baseline rules, so you subtract ½ from your true count. You get 4 (4½ − ½ = 4). Now, you multiply your unit bet by 4. Assuming you are playing a $25 unit, you should be betting $100 ($25 × 4 = $100).

Example 2. Your true count is now 3. Playing by the same rules, you again subtract. This time, you get a multiplier of 2½. You should multiply your unit bet by

2½. If you are playing a $100 unit, it is easy. You bet $250. If you are betting $25, you will probably not bet exactly 2½ times $25, because that would be $62.50 and not only would it be hard to find $2.50 in chips or coins, but you would most likely look strange and attract attention. So, just do some rounding and bet $60 or $65.

You will play in different casinos with different rules, and you need to know how these rules affect your chances of winning, so that you can adjust your bet correctly. The chart below gives a short list of some of the more common rules you will find at casinos today, along with the casino advantage factor they require.

Rule	Casino Advantage Factor
Dealer Hits Soft 17	½
Double after Splitting NOT allowed	½
Double with 10 or 11 ONLY	½
Player loses all splits/ doubles against dealer blackjack	½
No surrender available	½
Early surrender available	−1

Chart 31. Common Casino Rules

Example 1. You are in a casino where the dealer hits on soft 17. This rule gives the casino an extra advantage of about .25 percent (it's actually .20 percent, but we round the numbers to make the math less painful). Therefore, in addition to the ½ you will subtract for the casino's benchmark advantage, you also have to subtract another ½ for the advantage due to this rule. So, if the true count gets up to 4, you will subtract 1 (½ + ½) to get 3 and bet 3 times your unit bet.

Example 2. You are in a casino where you can only double when your first two cards make 10 or 11, but early surrender is available. You should be using the exact true count as your multiplier, because the casino advantage factor is zero (½ + ½ − 1 = 0). So, if the true count gets up to 4, you will bet four times your unit bet. (Congratulations on finding a casino with great rules to play.)

PICKING A UNIT BET

You should choose your unit bet before you start playing. You may want to adjust your unit bet after a session of blackjack. If you won a lot of money, you may want to start betting a higher unit or, more importantly, if you lost a lot of money, you will probably want to bet a lower unit.

How you decide what unit bet to play is a personal choice. There is no rule to tell you exactly what amount you should play. It is based on your tolerance for risk, your desire to win money, your comfort with large bets, and, most importantly, your bankroll.

How risk-averse are you? Card counting is not the same as gambling. While gambling means laying money on the line, with a chance of winning and a chance of losing, if you count cards and play correctly, you essentially remove the chance of losing. So you don't have to be a gambler to play blackjack. Maybe you just want to play some blackjack, have some fun, and win a little money, without risking much. Of course, if you have a big enough bankroll to withstand a losing streak and keep playing, and you have the time and access to keep playing, there really is only a very minimal risk of your losing any money at all. But if you are going to Las Vegas for a weekend or to a local casinofor a few hours, you certainly face a risk that you will lose money. The lower your unit bet, the less money you are putting at risk.

If you are learning how to count cards as a way to make yourself some money, then you will want to bet a high unit. In the long run, if you do it correctly, you will win money by counting cards. But the amount you win depends on the amount you bet, and in order to win a *lot* of money, you need to bet a lot of money. Although counting cards moves the edge from the casino's side to the player's side, the edge is still very small. For a casino, a very small edge is okay, because they are multiplying that edge by millions of gamblers betting billions of dollars, twenty-four hours a day, every day of the year. The casino's edge of less than one percent works out to quite a nice sum. But as one player with a finite number of playing hours in the day, your small edge requires a large bet to make substantial gains.

Another thing to think about when deciding your unit bet is the pressure you will face at the casino. As your unit bet goes up, your bets overall go up, and the more you bet, the more interested the casino will be in your wins and losses. It is certainly less important to look casual and play the role of a regular (non-counting) gambler if you are playing at a $5 minimum table, than it is if you are at a $100 minimum table with all the high-rollers. When you bet high, you attract attention, and when you attract attention, you will find there is much more pressure on your card-counting abilities. You need to do everything you normally do to count cards, but now you do it all under the watchful eyes of the pit bosses and the "eye in the sky." This may not seem like a problem, but you should ask yourself if you can handle the pressure. Many people have dreamed of being professional blackjack

players only to find that they didn't have what it takes to play at high stakes. Without a doubt, the rewards are greater (in winnings and comps) when you bet higher, but the mental effort may be too much.

Finally, the most important thing to think of when you choose your unit is your bankroll. How much money do you have to play with? The biggest mistake I see gamblers make is to play above where their bankroll allows them to play. How many times have you been at a blackjack table and seen someone walk up with one chip and put it down on the table to play one hand? What happens when they get an 11 and the dealer has a 6 showing? Without fail, they either just hit the hand because they can't afford to double, or they go into their pocket or purse for more money ("reaching for the lunch money," I call it). If they're just hitting that 11, they're giving up their edge to the casino on a hand they probably would have won twice as much on. If they're reaching for the lunch money and they lose, they're probably going without lunch the next day.

As you've learned, the probabilities will make you a winner over time, but there is also a chance you will lose five, six, twelve, or even twenty hands in a row before you make all of those losses back. Your bankroll protects you from those swings. So you should choose a unit bet that is small enough that you will not overextend your bankroll. You want to be able to cover a number of bets, in case you hit a losing streak. You also need to be able to cover all the splitting, re-splitting, and doubling you are going to be doing.

As a general rule, you should have at least 50 unit bets with you when you sit down at the table, though to be on the safe side it is best to have as much as 100 times your unit bet. When the count goes up, you'll find yourself betting three, four, even five times your unit bet on two hands at a time. That is why you need a lot of money with you for protection against down swings. For example, if you are going to Las Vegas for the weekend and you are bringing $5,000 with you to bet, a good number to play would be a $50 unit bet, and it would not be advisable to play any more than a $100 unit. Of course, you could feel pretty safe betting less than $50 units, if you wanted to lower your risk. If, by Saturday, you had ridden a hot streak and doubled your money to $10,000, you might think about increasing your unit bet. You would be able to cover a higher unit because you would have twice as much money with you. (Of course, had you lost $2,500 instead, you should do the smart thing and cut your unit bet, or you might find yourself going home with nothing.)

REVIEW QUESTIONS

Let's do some more card-counter math problems. For each situation given below, calculate the amount you should bet.

1. The true count is 5. Your unit bet is $20. The table is using the bench-mark rule set.
2. The true count is 9. Your unit bet is $100. The rules are the benchmark rules, but doubling is not allowed after splitting.
3. The true count is 2. Your unit bet is $50. The rules are the benchmark rules, but early surrender is available.
4. The true count is −1. Your unit bet is $100. The rules are the benchmark rules.
5. The true count is 11. Your unit bet is $10. The rules are the benchmark rules, plus surrender is not available, dealers hit soft 17, and doubling is not allowed after splitting.

AT THE TABLE

The most obvious sign that a player is counting cards is that he will go from a very small bet to a very large bet in the same shoe, sometimes as quickly as one hand later. If you were to exactly follow the strategy I've just given for betting, there would very likely be times you would do the same. You may have a very low count one hand, then see a run of small cards that increase the count. If there are few decks left, this will mean a big increase in the true count, and consequently, in your bet. If you were playing a large unit, the difference in the true count could make a very large difference in your bet (because it is multiplied). So, for example, you could find yourself going from a table minimum $25 bet to a bet of $400 each on two hands. This is liable to raise a red flag for a pit boss or other casino employee watching your play.

You may want to cut down on your "spread," the difference between your minimum and maximum bets. The easiest way to do this would be to cap your bet at a certain level. For example, you might play a $200 unit but cap your bet at $800. Therefore, even though you are playing a $200 unit bet and the true count gets as high as 7, you will still only place an $800 bet. Of course, this cuts down on the amount you expect to win, but winning a reduced amount for a long time is probably preferable to winning a very large amount once and then getting fingered as a card counter and barred from playing at that casino.

Professional card counters use other methods to reduce their spreads and allow them to play unnoticed for longer. These include call-ins, allowing the player to play only at high counts. Rather than capping the high bet, this increases the low bet (because the player will play only when he should be betting high), which also reduces the spread. Some professionals only play high counts, but flat-bet to avoid detection. This is not optimal, but is certainly safer (at least for a while).

You should take into account the attention you are getting from casino staff, as well as the amounts you are betting, to decide whether you feel you need to reduce your spreads. Although proportionally it is the same, a spread of $5 to $100 is clearly not the same as a spread of $50 to $1,000 or $500 to $10,000.

CHAPTER SEVEN

REFINING BASIC STRATEGY

Knowing the count helps you win at blackjack by knowing when you have the best chance of beating the dealer. It enables you to bet highest when you have the highest chance of winning and bet the least when your chance of winning is lowest. But there is a second advantage you can gain from your knowledge of the count. You can change the way you play hands based on your knowledge of what cards you (and the dealer) have the best chance of receiving.

I have taught you the "basic strategy" of playing blackjack. This is the mathematically-proven best way to play every possible hand if you don't have any knowledge of the cards remaining in the shoe. This strategy is certainly good enough to use to win money playing blackjack. Just playing according to basic strategy and betting according to the system laid out in the last chapter, you will gain an advantage over the casino, and in the long run, you will win money. However, if you want to increase your advantage even more, you can also use the count to adjust your playing strategy.

When you know the count, you know the relative odds that a high card (i.e., a 10 or an ace) will come out next. You can use this information to your advantage. For example, think of the situations where you have a hard 12 through 16. Even though you cannot possibly beat a dealer's hand with these totals, you will stand when the dealer has something lower than 7 showing, in hopes that he will bust and you will still win. What if you knew that there was a much lower chance of that happening than usual? You would be more likely to take a card when the dealer is less likely to bust (and the card is less likely to bust your hand, as well).

Example 1. You have 8♠ 4♣ and the dealer shows a 4♦. Basic strategy tells you to stand with a 12 against a 4. You expect the dealer to have 14 and end up busting, so you don't risk getting a 10 yourself and busting with 22. However, if your count is low, then there is less of a chance that the dealer will have that 14, leading to less of a chance that the dealer will end up busting. More importantly, there is less of a chance that you will bust when you take a card. Therefore, there must be a threshold at which it makes more sense to take a card yourself, instead of standing. In fact, if you run the numbers, you find that that threshold is where the count goes negative. What that means is, when the count is 0 or when the count is positive (meaning there are more high cards left than low cards), it is best to stand and hope the dealer busts. But when the count goes negative (meaning there are now more low cards left than high cards), it is actually best to take a card yourself. This is an adjustment to the basic strategy you can make if you count cards.

In fact, for every action listed in the basic strategy charts I've given you, there is a threshold at which it makes sense to do the opposite. In many cases, when the count is low, you will want to take a card rather than stand. When the count is high, you will want to stand rather than taking the chance of busting yourself. You may want to split pairs you wouldn't have normally. Or you may want to surrender hands that you wouldn't have normally, because the chances are so much higher that the dealer will beat you.

When we run the numbers, we find that there are several situations where the count should affect your strategy, though most of the strategies will never change. To take an extreme example, if you have a 9♥ J♦ but the dealer is showing a K♣, basic strategy tells you to stand because you already have 19. But there is still a threshold where the chance that the dealer has a 10 under that king is so high, it makes more sense to surrender. However, that threshold is so high, you will never see a count that high (especially when the casinos do not deal out all the cards before shuffling). So when I talk about adjusting the strategy according to the count, there are really only a few situations where you might change your strategy.

Below, I will discuss the most important adjustments to basic strategy that you will need to know. These situations are the most important because they come up more often than others and, more importantly, they will add the most to your expected win totals. In fact, although there are numbers you can learn for almost every possible situation, if you were to only memorize these few, you would gain most of the possible advantage from knowing the count. Because the other situations happen so infrequently and because the change in strategy won't help you win so many more hands, the other situations do little to increase your winnings.

INSURANCE

Earlier in this book, I told you that taking insurance is a bad bet. I showed you the numbers, which showed that the odds of there being a 10 underneath the dealer's ace are lower than the 2-to-1 odds the bet pays. But that assumed that you know nothing about the cards that are left in the shoe. When you have some knowledge about the odds that the next unseen card is a 10, you can make a more intelligent call on taking insurance.

Specifically, if there are more 10's left in the deck than usual, the odds may swing to a better than 2-to-1 chance that the dealer has insurance. This is when it is a winning bet to take insurance. Running the numbers, we get the number 3 as the threshold above which you should take insurance. (To be exact, the number is 2.9, but we round up to be safe and because you will not know the true count to such detail.)

When the true count is above 3, take insurance. This is the most important number you can learn. When the count is above 3, it means the chances are higher that anyone, including the dealer, will get a blackjack, so you will see this situation more than you think. And when it happens, you will have a big bet out, if you follow the correct betting scheme, so make sure to take advantage of insurance.

A quick note: The number is actually different for single- and double-deck blackjack games. In single-deck games, you should take insurance if the true count is higher than 1.5, and in double-deck games, when the true count is higher than 2.5. I won't include single- and double-deck numbers for other rules, but this one is important (and different) enough that I had to mention it.

16 VERSUS 10

Basic strategy says that you should surrender a 16 against a dealer's 10, and stand if surrender is not allowed or you have more than two cards. Therefore, the adjustments to basic strategy involve two separate numbers.

The first decision should be whether to surrender or not, provided it is available and you are in a position to use it. *You should surrender a 16 against a 10 for any true count higher than −2.* In most cases, you should not be playing if the true count is below −2, but at a crowded casino or if you are near the end of a shoe, you may be playing a poor count. If the count is below −2, you should take a hit on your 16, as you will see below. Note that you should not surrender a pair of 8s at negative counts (you should split), but you should surrender against positive counts.

If you cannot surrender (or if the count is below−2), the second decision is whether to hit or to stand. The threshold number for this decision is exactly 0, meaning *if the count is positive you stand and if the count is negative you hit.* A negative count means more low cards are left, so in this case you take a chance and hit your 16, hoping not to bust.

15 VERSUS 10

Fifteens against 10 represent the same decisions as 16 versus 10, but the numbers are different. *With a 15 against a dealer 10, you should surrender when the count is 0 or positive, but not when the count is negative.*

Basic strategy says to hit on 15 against a 10. But the decision number for standing versus hitting is +4. *You should stand with 15 against 10 when the true count is higher than 4.*

PLAYING 12s

You always see people agonizing about what to do when they have 12s. They hate to hit them, and they can't stand to stop with only 12. Perhaps that's reflected in the sensitivity of the playing strategy for 12s to the count. Basic strategy tells you to hit with 12 against 2 or 3, but stand against 4.

As I have already told you, *you should also hit with 12 against 4 when the count is negative.* When the count is negative, it means there are more low cards, which can't bust your hand when you only have 12. Conversely, when the count is positive, it means there are more 10s that will bust your hand. That's why, as the count goes up, you will start to stand even against low cards for the dealer. In fact, *when the count goes up to +2 or higher, you should stand with 12 against 3. When the count goes up to +3 or higher, you should also stand against a dealer showing 2.*

DOUBLING WITH 9

As the count goes up, you will double more often, because you have a better chance of catching the one card you need to make a great hand. Nines, especially, are sensitive to the count, because there are a few borderline cases where the odds hinge on the cards remaining to be played.

Basic strategy tells us we should only double with 9 against a dealer showing a 3 through 6. In fact, if the count goes up, we may also want to double against a 2 and even against a 7. *When the true count reaches 1, you should start to double with 9 against 2. You should only double with 9 against 7 when the count is equal to 3 or more.*

Just as you want to double more often when there are more 10s out there for you to catch, you will also want to double less when the odds are lower that you'll get that good card. That means that as the count goes down, you will stop doubling in some cases when you would have according to basic strategy. Specifically, *with a 9 against a 3, you should not double when the count is negative.* (You should just hit instead.)

DOUBLING WITH 10

Treat 10s the same as 9s when thinking of doubling. You will double more often as the count goes up, or conversely, less often when the count gets low.

You are already told to double with 10 against any dealer card except 10 or ace. When the count goes up to 4 or higher, you should also double against 10 and ace. In other words, *when the true count is 4 or higher, always double when you have 10.*

However, when the count goes down, you will double less often. *When the count goes below −1, do not double a 10 against a 9.* You will generally double with 10 against all cards lower than 9, regardless of the count. (That's because the threshold numbers at which you wouldn't double are so low, you shouldn't be playing at all with counts so low.)

DOUBLING WITH 11

With an 11, you are told to double against any dealer up-card except an ace. Well, when the count goes up, you will even double your 11 against an ace. *In fact, you should double with 11 against an ace when the count is only +1 or higher.*

Example. You get a 2♦ 9♦, but the dealer shows an A♠. First, you must decide whether to take insurance. Then, you must decide what to do with your hand. If the count is low, say −3, you will certainly not take insurance. You also won't want to double against an ace. You should just take a hit. What if the count was up to +2? In that case, you still would not want to take insurance. (Remember, the threshold for taking insurance is +3.) But you will double instead of taking a hit, because the count is higher than +1. If the count were anything higher than +3, you would take insurance and double. (That's when you cross your fingers, because you risk losing a lot of money if the dealer doesn't have blackjack but your double still doesn't work and you lose.)

SPLITTING 10s

Do you want to look like the biggest, baddest gambler in the world? It's easy to do. Just split 10s. You can split any pair of 10-valued cards, not just exact pairs. So, even if you have a jack and a king or a 10 and a queen, you can still split. Of course, almost no one ever does it, because that would mean throwing away a very strong hand of 20.

However, when the count gets very high, it sometimes actually makes sense to split your 10s. That's because the odds are so high that you will get 10s on top of each card, you will end up with two hands of 20, rather than just the one. This move is sure to draw a crowd and impress them greatly if it works out. (*Note:* It is also likely to draw casino personnel, who will be trying to decide if you are a crazy gambler throwing money away, or a pro

SPLITTING 10s AT THE TABLE

Although splitting 10s against a 5 or 6 when the count is very high is the right move to make, the dealer will certainly not be expecting you to do it. In fact, most dealers won't even ask what you want to do when you have a 20. They will fly right past your hand and go to the next person, or start on their hands.

Make sure you stop the dealer. Speak up as the dealer is looking at your cards, and you can stop him before he moves on. Or, you may want to place the chips next to your original bet to signify that you want to split before the dealer gets to your hand. That will at least confuse the dealer enough to stop and ask you what you want to do.

Of course, it is best if you do not get the pit boss involved, because you don't need any extra scrutiny of your play. In many cases, the dealer will tell the pit boss when someone splits 10s, but you may be able to get away without the pit boss noticing. If the pit boss does come over, you can feel free to try an acting job. Make yourself seem like a whimsical gambler, saying "I never tried this before" or "I had a crazy feeling" or something like that.

who's too good for them to beat. If they figure out that you're the latter, you are sure to get barred from the blackjack tables.)

In any case, splitting 10s is exciting and fun and can be valuable. *So, when the count gets to be +4 or higher, you should split 10s against a dealer showing 6. If the count gets to be +5 or higher, you should also split 10s against a 5.*

SUMMARY

I have given you a lot of different situations and numbers, and, once again, the only way for you to use them correctly is to memorize them completely. To make it a little easier, here is a chart of the above strategy adjustments, in order by count. Chart 32 starts with low positive numbers and gets higher. These are the numbers you will see the most, because lower counts happen more often and you will hopefully be playing mostly with positive counts. Below those, I've added the negative counts, as well.

WHEN THE COUNT IS . . .	YOU SHOULD . . .
0 or positive	Stand on 16 against 10
+1 or higher	Double 9 against 2
+1 or higher	Always double with 11
+2 or higher	Stand on 12 against 3
+3 or higher	Stand on 12 against 2
+3 or higher	Take insurance
+3 or higher	Double 9 against 7
+4 or higher	Stand on 15 against 10
+4 or higher	Always double with 10
+4 or higher	Split 10s against 6
+5 or higher	Split 10s against 5
Negative	Hit 12 against 4
Negative	Not double 9 against 3
Negative	Not surrender 15 against 10
Lower than −1	Not double 10 against 9
Lower than −2	Not surrender 16 against 10

Chart 32. A look at the strategy adjustments, in order of count

COMPLETE STRATEGY ADJUSTMENTS

As I've said, there are numbers for many more situations than the ones I've listed above. The others will not provide a huge lift, but they will increase your advantage, and who knows? Someday, you may find yourself playing with an A♥ 8♣ against a 2♠ and the true count at +9. Basic strategy says to stand, but you should double in that case.

If you are determined to know all of the strategy adjustment numbers, I've provided them (for the benchmark rule set) in Appendix G on *page 118*. However, I do not recommend you spend too much time memorizing every little number in the chart. In fact, your time would certainly be better spent practicing counting or even just playing. The increased advantage you will get from learning strategy adjustments is not big enough to make the time spent learning (and the risk of errors) worth the investment. You may be surprised to learn that even the MIT Blackjack Team, a famous and experienced team of professional blackjack players, does not require its players to know any of these numbers. They have found through experience that they weren't necessary to make money playing blackjack. Most of the advantage from counting cards comes from the betting strategy and not from the adjustments to the playing strategy.

REVIEW QUESTIONS

These questions are the same format as those found after the chapter on Basic Strategy, except now I will give you the true count as well. Use that information to decide what action the player should take.

1. Player: J♥ 3♦ 3♠   Dealer: K♣
   True Count: –2

2. Player: 4♣ 5♣   Dealer: 2♠
   True Count: 3

3. Player: 8♦ 3♠   Dealer: A♥
   True Count: 1½

4. Player: 5♠ 7♥   Dealer: 3♦
   True Count: 3

5. Player: 10♦ 5♥   Dealer: Q♠
   True Count: 4

6. Player: 6♣ 4♠   Dealer: A♦
   True Count: 6

7. Player: 3♥ 9♠   Dealer: 4♠
   True Count: –1

8. Player: J♣ 6♠   Dealer: J♥
   True Count: –2½

PUTTING IT ALL TOGETHER

Believe it or not, if you've read the entire book up to this point, you now know enough to change yourself from a sucker to a winner. You know how to play your hands, you know how to count cards, and you know how to use the information from that count to bet wisely and to change your play to improve your chances of winning. It is time to put it all together. Time to go to a casino and start winning money! This chapter explains how to do just that, including ways to improve your odds even further with some tricks at the casino.

STRAIGHT COUNTING

The obvious way to start making money is just to go to a casino, sit down at a table and start betting. You don't need to know anything special. Just use the knowledge you've gotten already in this book.

Sit down at any blackjack table. To improve your odds, find a table or a casino that offers favorable rules. Look for surrender to be available and dealers that stand on soft 17s. But even if you don't find those favorable rules, you can still win money. Just remember to adjust your count by the right amount when you choose your bet.

Before you start playing, you should figure out your unit bet, as described in Chapter 6. It goes without saying that you should also have practiced enough to be proficient at counting and at making correct strategy decisions on your hands.

Now, sit down at a table, preferably when the dealer has just finished shuffling. That will put you in the best position to know the count. If you miss a few rounds, just remember to add the cards you missed to the "remaining" decks, when you calculate your true count.

What follows is simply playing blackjack as I've described. Watch all the cards and keep the running count. Calculate the true count and use that to make your bet. If the count is negative, bet the table minimum. If the count is positive and high enough to offset the casino's advantage, use it to determine your bet. Then play your hand according to basic strategy, or, if you've studied hard, you can use the adjustments based on the count.

Remember that the count won't get high every single shoe. In fact, most of the time it will stay near 0, and many times it will go negative for the entire shoe. But if you choose to play this way, you must be patient and keep playing and keep counting until the count does go up and you can start to increase your bet. When the shoe ends and the dealer shuffles, put the running count back at 0 and start over. If you won a lot of money in that shoe, you may want to recalculate your unit bet because you can afford to bet higher. If you lost a lot of money in that shoe, you definitely should recalculate your unit bet, because you may not be able to afford to bet at the level you were betting before. If you don't recalculate your unit, you may wind up completely broke when the count finally turns positive.

JUMPING FROM TABLE TO TABLE

If you play blackjack exactly the way I described above, you will win money in the long run. But it will be a very difficult grind. You will play many hands when the casino has the advantage, waiting for those times when you have the advantage instead, and can bet higher. You will have to be very patient, and you will wait out long periods when your bankroll is low, you are losing, and you must just bet low and slowly win your money back. Counting cards doesn't guarantee you will never lose; only that, if you play enough hands, you will win in the end.

But there are ways of making your blackjack play more efficient. The best way to do that is to not play when the casino has the advantage. It is very easily done. You just sit down and play as described above, but this time, when the count goes negative, rather than betting the minimum and hoping to ride out the low count, you should get up and walk away. Do not play when the count is negative.

In this way, you cut down the hands that you play at the casino's advantage and increase the percentage of hands that you play with the edge for yourself. Obviously, your odds of winning are better. It will still take patience, and quite a bit of willpower to actually get up and leave the table when the count goes negative.

BACK-COUNTING

If you want to minimize the low-expectation hands even further, you can back-count for yourself and only sit down at a table when the count is high. Back-counting means standing next to a table and just watching the play and counting the cards without playing. In this way, you can simply watch a table when the count is low or negative, and, as soon as the count goes above a certain level (to the point where you have an advantage, or even higher if you are feeling very risk-averse), you can sit down and start playing. As long as you keep the correct count in your head while you watch, you can play correctly when you sit down, just as if you had been at the table the whole time.

By back-counting, you ensure that you will only play when the count is high, thus maximizing your odds of winning. This doesn't necessarily mean that you will win money any faster, because you may have to watch many shoes before you finally get one high enough for you to sit down and play. But you will avoid playing all those hands with a negative or low count, so your expected win rate will be higher.

In addition, some card counters use back-counting to disguise the fact that they are counting cards. That is because the most obvious sign of a card counter is someone starting by betting very low and then suddenly betting very high (when the count goes up). But if you back-count and only sit down and play when the count is already high, you will never play hands at a low count, so you will never bet a low amount. You will always be betting high, and the dealers and pit bosses will just think you are a big gambler who bets high all the time. Many casinos now don't allow you to enter mid-shoe.

COMPS AND HEAT

Most people who start to think about betting high and playing a lot in big casinos also start to dream about the food and drink and the rooms the casino will

AT THE TABLE

There are tricks you can use to get out of playing hands when the count is negative and the casino has the advantage. If you are near the end of the shoe, or you are in a crowded casino and don't want to lose your seat, you can try these instead of getting up and leaving the table.

You can always just choose not to play a round or two. Just do not bet and when the dealer asks (they usually stop and let you bet, thinking you forgot to ante) say you choose not to play that round. If you want an excuse, say you want to change your luck (which works best if you've just lost one or two hands). It is perfectly reasonable to stay out of a couple rounds. You will not be asked to leave unless you skip many hands in a row. It is normal to quit a shoe and say you will wait until the shuffle, provided it may be coming soon.

If the count goes negative early in the shoe, and you can't just skip a few rounds, that may be the perfect time for nature to call. You can ask the dealer to save your spot while you go to the bathroom (or to make a phone call or check on your spouse or any other excuse). A dealer won't mind saving a spot for you for a few minutes. If the casino is crowded and people are waiting to sit at the table, someone may borrow your spot while you're gone, but you should get it back when you return. Now you can step out for a couple minutes and miss a very negative shoe. If you're very good, you'll time your absence to return just in time for the dealer to finish shuffling the new shoe.

Here is a simple rule of thumb: *If, after one deck has already been dealt, the true count is below −1, you should stop playing that shoe.* When it gets that low, it may still turn around and start to go up, but chances are that won't happen. Or, if it does, it will happen so late that you will not get many hands with an edge. You are better off finding another shoe to play, in case the count goes up on it.

In fact, this is the way many card counters who work alone do it. They simply play shoes until the count goes negative, at which point they get up and find a different table with a new shoe starting. Obviously, to do that, you need to be in one of the larger casinos that have several blackjack tables with many open spots for you to sit down at. You should usually be able to find that in a place like Las Vegas or Atlantic City, but it may be harder to find in an isolated casino somewhere.

By jumping around and starting as many new shoes as possible during your time in the casino, you can maximize the number of high-count shoes you play, while minimizing the number of hands you play when the casino holds the advantage. And that is a sure way to increase your expected winnings.

give them for free. Just because when you count cards, you are doing something the casinos would not like if they knew about it, does not mean that you can't earn some comps while you do it. Some players choose to pass on all comps and just try to play "under the radar" and never even get noticed by the pit bosses. Others will take whatever they can get from casinos, for as long as they can until they get caught counting. Professionals cut down on expenses greatly by letting the casinos pay for their rooms, their meals, even their flights to and from Las Vegas.

Whether you choose to try to get comped will affect the way you may play. Comps are given to players based on the casino's expected gain from the players. That means, they take your average bet and multiply that by the time you spend playing to figure the total amount they expect to win from you. Only at certain levels will you receive comps. In order to earn comps for yourself, you will have to play consistently for extended periods of time, or for big money, and you will have to be visible to the casino.

In order to be visible, you will have to get "rated," meaning you give the casino some information to track you by. Usually, just a name (be it your real name or not) and a birth date (again, real or not) is enough to get a player's card, which is then used to track your play. Whenever you sit down to play, you can show your card and, in this way, accumulate your play until you reach the right levels to ask for comps. But that means that you will want to sit down in front of a pit boss and be seen. You will probably need to sit at one table, or at least be very visible at whatever you table you move to, so you get credited for all your play. It makes it very difficult to jump in and out of shoes and still get credited for your play.

In addition, if you prefer to back-count and only play high counts, the casino may mistake you for the type of player who only plays a few hands but hopes to get comped for the value of consistent play. Pit bosses may expect you to play for longer periods of time if you are not consistently playing every hand in a shoe.

Of course, when you invite a pit boss to watch your play, in order to determine if you are worthy of complimentary food or rooms, you are also inviting the pit boss to study how you play. You are simply asking for "heat." Heat is when you are being watched because you are suspected of counting cards. Professionals can sense heat from casino personnel and usually know when to stop playing before the heat gets so hot that they get "burned out," or thrown out of the casino. If you are a low-stakes player just hoping to get a free buffet, you probably don't have to worry about heat too much, but when you invite a pit boss to count your bets and your winnings, it may just be an invitation to catching you counting cards, if you are not skilled at disguising your play.

SHUFFLE TRACKING

Shuffle tracking is an advanced method card counters use to take advantage of good cards. Simply put, by tracking where certain "clumps" of cards go when the dealer shuffles, a card counter can cut the cards to give himself the greatest advantage, or to know when his advantage will be high (even without counting).

How does it work? Watch the dealer shuffle next time you are at a casino. Dealers are taught a certain way to shuffle, and they follow that method exactly every time. When shuffling a six-deck shoe, for example, they generally split the shoe into several piles, then riffle two piles together and set them aside, until they have shuffled all six decks together again. However, this method of shuffling certainly doesn't guarantee a completely random shuffle. (Mathematicians have even done studies and written papers proving that point.) In fact, it keeps many of the cards together in general areas of the shoe, though it perhaps moves them from one area of the

AT THE TABLE

What is the best way to disguise the fact that you are counting cards? You can bet differently from how the count tells you to, but then you are giving up the advantage that counting gives you. You can make some playing errors to look like you don't know what you're doing, but then you might as well just give the casino a piece of your winnings, and the margins are thin enough as it is.

The best way to disguise your play is by your personality. There is a definite stereotype of a card counter. It is a very quiet, solitary card player, focused entirely on the cards and what is going on inside his mind. This type of card counter will attract a pit boss's attention, who will be able to anticipate the player's moves.

If, instead, you are chatting with fellow players, making jokes, and acting friendly toward the dealer and even the pit boss, you will probably not be suspected as a card counter. Of course, the ability to keep the count and make calculations in your head while keeping up a conversation takes practice, but it is worth it. Be confident. Call a pit boss over and ask about the best restaurant in the casino or the best show on the strip. What pit boss would suspect a card counter who actually invites him over to his table while he plays?

If the pit boss is a little too focused on you, you could just bring your own friends along when you play. Even if they don't play themselves, you can talk to them and enjoy yourself, while basically using them as cover for your card counting. I have personally spent time just hanging out at high-stakes tables in Vegas, acting as cover for professional card counter friends. Not only does it reduce heat, it makes the game more fun.

shoe to another. The point is, by watching the dealer shuffle, an experienced card player can track where a group of cards starts and where it ends up.

Now, if during play of a shoe, you notice that at one point the count is around zero, then within a couple rounds has gone down to −12, you know that there were a large number of high cards in that small area of the shoe. When those cards get discarded, they stay in the same area of the discard pile. Regardless of whether you won your hands or not at that time, you know that a preponderance of high cards in a small area of the shoe means a big advantage for you. If you can track that area of the shoe through the shuffle and see where it ends up in the new

(shuffled) shoe, you can use that knowledge to your advantage. If you hold the cut card, you can cut the shoe directly before that clump of cards. That means those cards will be the first to come out in the new shoe. Which means you have a known advantage for at least the first couple rounds of the new shoe. Bet high and take advantage.

Conversely, if you know where there is a clump of low cards (in other words, an area of the shoe where the count when way up), and you are cutting, you can greatly help yourself. Simply cut directly after that clump of low cards in the shoe. When the dealer moves those cards to the back of the shoe, they will be the set of cards that never get dealt at the end of the shoe. Your shoe will start with a high count, rather than a count of zero. Again, you can bet high from the start, and, if the rest of the cards fall right, the count may only get higher from there.

Shuffle tracking is certainly a less exact science than standard card counting, but for an experienced player, who has benefited from watching hundreds of shuffles and gains a kind of innate understanding of high- versus low-count sets of cards, it can be a very profitable method.

ACE TRACKING

Ace tracking is similar in concept to shuffle tracking. But, as the name suggests, rather than track an entire set of cards, the objective is to track aces and know exactly when an ace will be coming out of the shoe. Again, the nonrandom shuffle is to be thanked for the existence of ace tracking. Because the cards are placed into the discard rack in the exact order they are dealt, a series of 4♥ 9♦ A♠ will remain in that order when discarded. When the shoe is shuffled, though the cards get riffled together from various places in the deck, the shuffle is not complete. Usually, the cards in one area of the shoe will only get riffled together once or twice. (The casino can't lose all that valuable betting time while the dealer shuffles obsessively to make it a completely random shuffle.) The sequence will often remain together when the (shuffled) cards are returned to the shoe.

When the cards are played, the player simply watches for the sequence to know when an ace will be coming out. With very good luck, the first couple cards in the sequence will be the last cards to be played in one round. That means the ace will turn out to be the first card out of the shoe for the next round, and a player sitting at first base can make a huge bet knowing he will be receiving an ace. (As I have said, the ace is the most valuable card for the player. It increases the player's edge by much more than card counting ever would.)

Not only is ace tracking very profitable, because of the huge advantage to the player who gets an ace, but it is also valuable for disguising the play of a card counter. The ace could come up at any time, unrelated to a high or low count. That means that the player could be placing a very large bet when the count is low. Casino personnel watching that play will certainly be thrown off the trail of a card counter. (It would take very close consideration and multiple shoes before any pit boss could finger a player for tracking aces and, by that time, the player would surely have won a lot of money.)

COUNTING ALTERNATIVE BLACKJACK GAMES

If you are wondering if the alternative blackjack games discussed in these pages—Spanish 21, Double Exposure, Multiple-Action Blackjack—can be counted just like standard blackjack, the answer is yes and no. All of the games can be counted, and the count can be used to increase the player's chances of winning. However, the counting often must be done using alternative methods to match the game's rules, or the standard counting system can be used but is not as effective.

Spanish 21 is a game that was invented in part to prevent card counters from gaining an advantage on the casino. This was done very simply. The four 10s were removed from each deck. Think what that does to the count. Assume, instead of the 10s having been removed from the deck, they were simply the first four cards dealt in the deck. After those four cards are dealt, the count would be −4. Multiply that by six decks, as most Spanish 21 games are played with a six-deck shoe, and you find that you start with a running count of negative 24. Of course, there are many cards left in the shoe and it's possible the next 24 cards will all be low cards, evening the count. But clearly, it is more difficult for the count to turn positive in Spanish 21 than it is in standard blackjack. If you want to put in the time and count shoe after shoe at a Spanish 21 table for the slim chance that a high count will emerge, it is perfectly acceptable. But if you consider your time valuable and want to reduce the number of shoes you must play and increase the amount you are expected to win, you are obviously better off playing standard blackjack.

Double Exposure Blackjack requires a very different basic strategy (and different strategy adjustment numbers, if you want to go that far), but it can be counted using the standard high-low counting system. In fact, the rules of Double Exposure make it even more sensitive to changes in the relative number of high and low cards. In other words, a count of 4 in a Double Exposure game means an even higher advantage for the player than a count of 4 in standard blackjack. The difference is not great enough to cause you to change your betting strategy, but it should reassure you, if you want to put in the time to learn the basic strategy for Double Exposure Blackjack.

Because Multiple-Action Blackjack uses the same rules and the same basic strategy as standard blackjack, it can also be counted in the same way. In fact, there is even some advantage to playing Multiple-Action Blackjack when counting cards. It makes it easier to increase your bet when the count goes up. There is no rule in Multiple-Action Blackjack that you must play all three bets, so it is possible to wait out a low count with only one bet per hand, then, when the count gets high, to jump in with three bets and take advantage of the high count before it goes down again. This can be useful not only for getting more bets in when there is a high count (which you should be doing anyway, if there are empty spots at your blackjack table), but also for disguising the spread in your betting. In addition, when the count goes low, you may want to spread your bet to three spots, to try to get more cards dealt in hopes that the count will go back up. Of course, if there are other players at your table and they are playing three bets, you need not even bet three times your own money at the low count. (The dealer will have to play three hands for the other player, no matter whether you bet or not.)

Finally, the side bets can even be counted, but these will generally require a special counting system. The Over/Under bet can be counted quite effectively, as would be expected. However, the standard high-low count does not work well for this bet, because it counts the ace as a "high" card, when it counts as only 1 for this side bet. Instead, to count the Over/Under bet would require counting aces as low and keeping an entirely different count. If you are a math savant, and can keep both counts in your head, then you will be able to win a lot of money, but otherwise, I suggest sticking to the standard blackjack card counting and staying away from the side bets.

PLAYING WITH A TEAM

So, you've been playing for a while and you've been winning. You're an expert at counting cards and you never make any mistakes. But still you're not making much money at it. For one thing, there is the old adage that it takes money to win money, and you just don't have enough to bet big. Also, there just aren't enough hours in the day (or in the weekend, if it's just a quick trip to Las Vegas) to play enough to flatten the ups and downs and win consistently.

There is a solution that many entrepreneurial card counters have found: form a blackjack team. There are many advantages to playing in a team. First, a team can pool its money, creating a large bankroll and enabling very large bets (and, therefore, very large wins). Second, working with a team, you can make your play more efficient, playing only the most advantageous conditions and, thus, winning more money in less time. In addition, more people on a team means more man-hours for playing. Third, a team can play longer without getting caught. While a solitary card counter is very likely to draw attention after playing for many hours and winning, a blackjack team can use various tactics to disguise its play and can also shuffle personnel to avoid detection.

Although I do not recommend anyone try to form a professional blackjack team—it is difficult to manage, recruit, and train a team of players, and the risks are immense—I will provide the basics of team play. Team members do not simply join up, go out and play blackjack individually, and then meet and split up their winnings. If they did, it would reduce risk, enable longer play, and probably produce more winnings in the long run, but that is not getting the true power out of playing with a team. In fact, teams win by working together, not individually. These are some of the methods that teams use to win money and to avoid detection by the casinos.

BACK-COUNTING CALL-INS

The key to a card-counting team's winnings is the ability to play in only the most advantageous conditions. This is what an individual card counter does when he jumps from table to table, playing only when the count goes up and leaving when the count goes negative. And it is even more so when a player stands behind the table and counts, only playing when the count is high.

That is exactly what teams do, but they have multiple people to do the back-counting for them. A typical scheme will involve a small team of players attacking the same blackjack pit (or set of tables within the casino). One (or maybe two) of the players will be the "big player." He is the one who will come in with large amounts of money and make huge bets when the count is high. The rest of the players on the team will only be "spotters."

The spotters will stand around and watch the tables. When a dealer shuffles, a spotter will start to watch the cards and will keep the count. If the count goes negative, the spotter can just walk away and find another table where the dealer is shuffling and start over. If, on the other hand, the count goes up and starts to get high, the spotter will "call-in" the big player. This can be done with some kind of signal from the spotter. It needs to be a signal that the big player can recognize from far enough away, but also something that seems completely natural and wouldn't draw any attention from casino personnel. Teams have used things like different ways of standing, ways of holding one's arms, or gestures like scratching one's nose or rubbing one's ear. These are things that never get noticed unless someone is actually looking for them.

When the big player sees the signal, he will walk over to the spotter and the spotter will pass him the count. Again, this transfer needs to be done discreetly. It can be done with some sort of code. You can make up your own code. The key is just to say a word or to make a gesture that the big player can easily decode into the actual running count. (*Note:* The spotter passes the running count, not the true count, to maintain enough detail for the big player to make correct decisions as the shoe continues.)

PLAYING CALL-INS

Of course, it won't always look right for the spotters to be standing around watching the action at the tables. In high-stakes pits, it is often intimidating, if not discouraging, to stand and watch the play. There are also times when the casino is not crowded, and spotters standing around, signaling, and passing code words and information to big players can really stand out. For these times, it may make sense for the call-ins to be made by someone who is actually playing at the table.

In this case, the system works the same way as before, but now the spotter is sitting at the table playing. There will still be some sort of signal that the big player can see even though the spotter is sitting down at a table. It could be the way the spotter leans on the table, or the way he stacks his chips, or something like that. The spotter will call in the big player, again passing the count to the big player (which can be very tricky when you are both sitting at a table in plain view of the dealer and the pit boss). And as the big player picks up the play, betting high, the spotter moves on to a new table.

Of course, the spotter should be just playing the minimum bet for that table, for two reasons. First, the spotter will probably be playing poor counts, while waiting for the count to get high enough to call in the big player. So while the spotter plays at a disadvantage, he should play for low amounts, so it doesn't hurt the overall team edge as much. Second, the spotter does not want to look like a card counter by varying his bet with the count. The last thing a team needs is for a spotter to draw attention from the pit boss just before the big player comes in with the big money.

Because the spotters are playing at low counts when the casinos have the advantage, this system is less efficient than call-ins from back-counting spotters, who aren't losing any money. But it is not always possible to spot with back-counters alone, so you should have a system in place for calling in big players from the table.

AT THE TABLE

How can a person walk up to another person and receive a piece of information from that person without the dealer and pit boss standing right there ever knowing anything happened? It is easier than it seems. A casino is a very loud place, and words spoken softly can only be heard by people in the very immediate area. So, it is possible that a spotter could simply say the running count aloud to the big player.

But it is generally safer to create a code, so that even if the code is heard, it is not immediately obvious what the information means. A code is easy to form. Just think of the numbers. You will probably need a code word for each number from 2 or 3 up to 20, at least. Maybe you know the TV channel lineup in your area very well—if MTV is on channel 8 and ESPN is on channel 12, you have code words for 8 and 12. Maybe you remember your teachers' names from grades 1 through 12. As long as everyone memorizes the codes, it doesn't matter what you use (although it is better to use words that won't draw attention if heard at the casino—i.e., ESPN is better than Ms. Radziewycz).

You might even try a non-verbal code. The big player could walk up and stand directly in front of the spotter. The spotter could then tap the big player. Maybe taps on the right shoulder represent numbers from 11 to 15, while taps on the left shoulder represent numbers from 6 to 10. It seems a little risky, but probably could be perfected with some practice.

Once the big player has the running count, he can take over the counting. He will sit down at the table and start playing, betting high because the count is already high, but adjusting his bet (and possibly his play, as well) according to the count. The pit boss will not suspect the big player, because every time he sits down he bets high, and the variation in his bets is not great.

Meanwhile, the spotter has moved on to watch a new table. While the big player plays his big shoe, he can watch his spotters, in case they come upon another high count. If the count on the table he is playing goes down, the big player can leave or move to a table where another spotter is calling him in.

BIG PLAYERS WHO DON'T COUNT

Another way teams manage to bet high without getting caught is by teaming up on one table. What some teams will do is have spotters play at tables and call in big players, just as described above. However, when the big player comes to the table, the spotter never passes the count. Instead, he remains at the table, keeping the count himself, and signaling the big player exactly how to bet.

It is very easy for the big player to look natural in this case, because he isn't counting at all. He is just looking across the table to see how much to bet. In some cases, the big player will just bet a flat big bet, in order to not look like a card counter at all. The spotter will only signal the big player when to sit down and play and when to get up and leave (when the count has gone down).

This is a very difficult system for the casinos to figure out. One player (the spotter) is on one side of the table, betting table minimums every time, so that person is clearly not a counter. Another player (the big player) joins the table betting high, and keeps his bets high. At the same time, he's talking to the dealer and the other players and not seeming to pay any attention to anyone's cards but his own. Clearly, he is not counting, either. Only after the big player wins consistently for several sessions, and the "eye in the sky" realizes the same few people always seem to be at the table with him, will the casino realize it may have a blackjack team on its hands. By then, the team has gotten away with thousands of dollars, even hundreds of thousands.

INTERVIEW WITH A PRO

If you've read this whole book, and you practice hard, you will be able to win consistently at blackjack. You may be thinking that if you play enough blackjack, for enough money, you won't need to ever work a real job again. You can become a professional card counter.

But what does it mean to be a professional? How much money do you need? Should you go it alone, or form a team of card counters? What are the advantages and disadvantages of playing full-time? To answer some of these and other questions, I spoke with a working professional. Nick MacDonald (not his real name, of course) has been playing blackjack professionally for about ten years and has not held any other job for all of that time. He continues to play with one of the most well-known, and well-respected, blackjack teams today. Nick agreed to answer my questions about playing blackjack for big money. We also spoke about the advantages and disadvantages of betting big dollars (getting great gifts from casinos, but running the risk of getting kicked out). Finally, Nick gave some good advice for aspiring professionals.

ON LEARNING TO COUNT

Josh Hornik: How did you get started playing blackjack?

Nick MacDonald: Some friends of mine were on a blackjack team and they took me to a team meeting.

JH: And they taught you how to count cards?

NM: At the team meetings, which were really team practices, they would teach it. They started out with basic strategy, then counting, then bet calculations. The more advanced players would typically deal to the newer players. That's how part of the training would take place.

JH: You've been doing it for 10 years now. Do you still practice counting cards?

NM: Well, whenever I'm going to go on a trip [to a casino to play blackjack], I practice—to make sure I'm not rusty. Also, sometimes I will learn a new technique or read about something new, and I will practice that.

JH: So what do you do to practice?

NM: I'll deal to myself. I deal just as a dealer would deal in the casino. And I'll just be watching TV or something and, at the same time, counting the cards. I'll deal pretty fast and then stop every so often and check the count to see if I have it right.

JH: What about betting? Do you practice that?

NM: I'll usually pick a unit to bet, and while I deal to myself, I'll practice betting in my head. I'll deal really fast. Sometimes I will stop and calculate the exact optimal bet, and check that I had it right.

JH: What do you think is the single best way to practice card counting?

NM: Have someone experienced deal to you—someone who can deal exactly like a casino dealer, except faster. This type of person—someone who deals, flips the cards, and rakes them, exactly like in a casino—is difficult to find. He/she can also monitor your card-counting accuracy and give you pointers along the way. Nowadays it doesn't take me too long to get my skills sharp again if I haven't played for a while. When I first got started and was practicing alone, I would come up with all sorts of drills to get faster and more accurate.

ON PLAYING BLACKJACK

JH: You currently play on a professional blackjack team. How many people are there on your team?

NM: It's a little smaller than it used to be, but it's probably about 10 to 12 active members now.

JH: And how many of those will usually play together at one time?

NM: Typically about four.

JH: How do you find new people to join the team?

NM: We try to recruit friends and family members—people we know well and trust already.

JH: What traits do you look for in people, to make the best card counters for your team?

NM: We want someone who doesn't have a huge ego. We can't have people who think they know more than you about how to play blackjack. They have to be dependable—have a good work ethic. They also have to be good at following directions and work well in a team environment. On occasion we've had players who had problems following directions—probably due to their ego.

JH: Does their motivation matter—why they want to play on the team?

NM: Yes. I don't want people who just want to do it for the money. That could lead to early disappointment and frustration for them. You want someone who is intrigued by the game and how to beat it. I like when players are excited about what they are doing.

JH: So, once someone is on your team, how do you know they're any good at counting?

NM: We deal to them, and watch how they play and how they look when they play—if they look casual [while they're counting]. We've only ever had one or two people we had to ask to stop playing with us because they weren't progressing. A few others left on their own.

JH: How do the people on your team make money?

NM: Everyone gets paid a percentage of what they generate at the tables. It's not by what they actually win or lose, but by how much they are expected to win. When we break the bank [hit the target win amount and pay winnings out to investors], if we have made extra, we also distribute bonuses to players on the team.

JH: How do you choose where to play?

NM: Usually we go to the casinos with the best rules and the best limits. If you're with a team, you need a casino with high limits. And obviously, you need a place where your players aren't burnt [banned from playing blackjack].

JH: What is your favorite place to play blackjack?

NM: Probably the Mirage and Bellagio [in Las Vegas].

JH: How much do you usually bet when you play blackjack?

NM: If I'm playing the role of the big player, I think my average bet is about

$1,000 on each of two hands. It might be a little more.

JH: How much money do you have with you at the table, to bet that amount?

NM: Between $50,000 and $100,000 on hand. There are times when it's a lot more than that.

JH: What is the biggest bet you ever made on one hand?

NM: Well, the maximum bet in Las Vegas is $10,000. I've made that bet lots of times.

JH: What about the first time? Did you win?

NM: The first time? I can't really remember, but I probably won. [Laughs.]

JH: What is the highest amount you ever won in one blackjack session?

NM: About $115,000 to $120,000. That was over about three or four hours.

JH: What's the most you ever lost in one session?

NM: Around $70,000.

JH: Do you ever tip the dealer?

NM: Our team policy is to never tip, with one exception: if the dealer makes an error [in the player's favor], you can tip out of that money. But tipping really isn't necessary. When you look at the real (non-counting) high rollers—some of them are really cheap. They don't all tip.

JH: Speaking of team policy, do you ever drink while you play?

NM: Not when I'm playing for the team. Drinking definitely makes a difference. That's why we have a strict rule—no drinking when you're playing [for the team].

ON GETTING COMPS
AND GETTING KICKED OUT

JH: Do you get comps from the casinos you play at?

NM: Of course. Yes.

JH: What kind of things do you get?

NM: Everything. Room, food, drinks, shows, airfare, gifts from the gift shop. They'll give high rollers anything.

JH: What is the best comp you ever got from a casino?

NM: Once, the casino flew us to see the Super Bowl. Another time, the casino flew me on a ski vacation in Aspen.

JH: Have you ever been caught counting cards and barred from playing blackjack?

NM: Of course.

JH: How many casinos would you say you have been kicked out of?

NM: Hmm . . . Let me think. Probably around 25.

JH: How do they do it when they kick you out?

NM: Usually, I'll be playing blackjack and they'll send someone down and he'll come over and tap me on the shoulder and tell me I can't play blackjack anymore. Usually they're pretty courteous, but sometimes they try to intimidate you. They bring security guards with them. Lots of times, I see it coming and I leave [before they bar me]. They will always say something like "It's a management decision," rather than telling you the real reason they're doing it.

JH: Have you ever been physically threatened when you were kicked out?

NM: Not really. A couple of times, they've said something like "You're lucky there are people around," but that's about it.

JH: When you get kicked out, do you have to pay back your comps?

NM: No. Once in a while, they try to charge you for it, but we have usually been able to contest it. Most of the time, they don't even try.

JH: Do you use your own name when you play?

NM: Very, very rarely. It's just too easy for them to look it up.

JH: Do you wear disguises to avoid getting tagged as a known card counter?

NM: I've changed my look—different hair styles, different clothing, wearing glasses. I haven't worn serious disguises—wigs or prosthetics or something like that. But I've been to places that should know me and just put on a pair of glasses and they're like "Who are you?" [Laughs.]

JH: Do you ever change the way you play blackjack to try to keep from being caught?

NM: Yes, but minimally because you give up some of your edge [if you play non-optimally as a cover]. It's usually better to just stop playing if you start getting heat.

SOME FINAL ADVICE

JH: Do you consider yourself a gambler?

NM: No.

JH: Do you ever play any other casino games besides blackjack?

NM: No. I've played slots just as a cover when I'm spotting for another team member, but I haven't played for myself.

JH: Is playing blackjack fun for you?

NM: Yes, I really like it. In spite of the stress, when you're counting and betting high, it really is fun.

JH: Even when you're losing?

NM: It's not as fun, obviously, but it's still cool to do it. Even when I lose, I know [in the long run] I'm making money.

JH: What do you think is the hardest part of counting cards?

NM: Just putting it all together. Being able to do everything accurately and quickly and not looking like you're doing it. Also, dealing with the pressure at the casino.

JH: Last question. What advice do you have for someone who is just starting to count cards?

NM: Don't quit your day job. Start it off as a hobby. If you get really good, you can build up your bankroll, but you need a lot of money to make money at blackjack. Practice a lot—more than you think you need to. If you know an experienced card counter, have him deal to you. Be very patient. It's a grind.

GLOSSARY

ACE: A card whose value can be either 1 or 11, depending on the situation. The ace is the most powerful card in the deck in blackjack.

BACK-COUNT: To stand behind the players at a blackjack table and count the cards as they are played. By back-counting, you can wait until the count is high before you risk any of your money. This method is also frequently used in team play.

BARRED: Not allowed to play blackjack at that casino.

BASIC STRATEGY: The set of actions that give the player the absolute best chance of winning in every situation, assuming no knowledge of cards that have already been played.

BIG PLAYER: On a blackjack team, the player who bets the big money when called into a high-count shoe.

BLACKJACK: Another name for the game 21; or, a hand composed of an ace and a ten, jack, queen, or king, which usually pays 3-to-2 odds.

BURN CARD: The single card that the dealer discards before beginning to deal a new shoe. At some casinos, dealers burn more than one card.

BURN OUT: A term for getting thrown out of a casino, or barred from play, for being a suspected card counter.

BUST: Going over 21 with your hand. When you bust, you lose. When the dealer busts, you win, unless you're already busted.

"CHECKS PLAY": In most casinos, the dealer will call out "checks play" to alert the pit boss when any player bets more than $100 on a single hand. The "checks" in "checks play" refers to the black $100 "checks," or chips, used to "play" that hand.

COMPS: Free gifts from the casino, to entice you to play there. Comps include things like free food and drink or free rooms at the casino's hotel.

"(THE) COUNT": When a person talks about "the count," he/she is usually referring to the relative count of high cards versus low cards, and not to the true count.

COUNTING CARDS: The only way to give yourself the edge over the casino when playing blackjack. Usually refers to the act of both keeping the running count and betting according to the count to maximize your winnings.

CUT CARD: The plastic card, frequently yellow, that the dealer uses to cut the cards and to alert him/her to the need to shuffle toward the end of a shoe, as well as to hide the bottom card in the pack.

DEALER: The person who manages the cards and bets, and who plays a hand that you must beat to win.

DECK: A standard 52-card pack of cards. Blackjack is played in casinos with anywhere from one to eight decks.

DISCARD RACK: The clear plastic rack, found at the far left side of the table, where the dealer piles all used cards in a round. As the discard rack fills, the shoe empties. Either can be used to estimate the number of decks unseen.

DOUBLE: To double the bet on your hand, taking only one additional card.

DOUBLE DOWN: Another term for double.

DOUBLE EXPOSURE BLACKJACK: A game where the dealer turns both of his/her cards face up before the players play their hands.

EARLY SURRENDER: This rule allows the player to give up half of his/her bet before the dealer checks his hand for blackjack, enabling the player to save half his/her bet even when the dealer has blackjack.

"EVEN MONEY": A term used to describe taking insurance when the player has a blackjack. In this case, either the player wins his bet on insurance or wins 3:2 odds on his blackjack but loses his insurance, so the player gets paid "even money" whether the dealer has blackjack or not.

EXPECTED WIN: The amount that, if you play optimally, you would be mathematically expected to win.

FIRST BASE: The seat at the far right of the table, which is the first to play in a round.

GORILLA: Another word for the player in a blackjack team who bets high and plays but does not count the cards. Instead, the gorilla receives signals from a teammate, telling him what to bet.

HARD HAND: A hand that includes an ace, where the ace must be equal to 1, in order to keep the hand alive. (See soft hand.)

HEADS-UP: A head-to head play with the dealer. No other players are involved.

HEAT: Attention from casino personnel, such as a pit boss who suspects you of card counting.

HIGH–LOW COUNT: Another term for the relative count.

HIGH ROLLER: A big gambler, who plays for high stakes.

HIT: To take another card.

HOLE CARD: The dealer's card that is left face down and not shown to the players until they have all completed their hands.

INSURANCE: A bet that pays 2:1 odds if the dealer has blackjack. Since the bet is usually equal to half of the player's original bet, it essentially "ensures" the bet against the dealer's having blackjack.

LATE SURRENDER: The rule that allows the player to give up half of his bet and quit his hand, but only after the dealer has checked his hand for blackjack.

MULTIPLE–ACTION BLACKJACK A variation on blackjack in which the player can play up to three bets on each hand, while the dealer plays three separate hands using the same up card but different hole cards.

NATURAL: Another word for a blackjack.

OVER–UNDER: A side bet used at some blackjack tables, that allows the player to bet whether his first two cards will total over or under 13.

PAIR: Any two cards of the same value. Pairs also include any two cards that both equal 10 in value, including tens, jacks, queens, and kings.

PIT BOSS: The casino employee who watches a set of tables, keeping an eye on how much money is being won and lost, and who is playing. The pit boss is the most likely person to scrutinize your play for clues that you are counting cards.

PLAYER: The person who is betting money and trying to beat the dealer.

PUSH: A tie, occurring when the player and the dealer finish their hands with the same totals. This term may also be used when two equal bets are played—one winning and the other losing.

RELATIVE COUNT: The count of how many low cards you have seen, relative to the number of high cards you have seen. It is the same as the running count.

ROUND: A round of blackjack consists of each player at the table playing his/her hand, followed by the dealer completing his hand and paying out the winners.

RUNNING COUNT: The count of how many low cards you have seen, relative to the number of high cards you have seen. Same as the relative count.

SHOE: The box in which the dealer places the cards and deals cards out of. Also, the word for the series of hands played from one shuffle to the next.

SOFT HAND: A hand that includes an ace, where the ace is equal to 11, leaving the flexibility to take any card without busting.

SPLIT: Double your bet, and split one hand consisting of a pair of the same value cards into two separate hands of one card each.

SPOTTER: A blackjack team player who watches the count and calls other players into hot shoes.

STAND: To stop playing your hand, leaving it at its current value.

SUCKER: Someone who plays a game of chance that is weighted against him, making it impossible to win in the long run.

SURRENDER: To give up your hand, keeping half of your bet.

THIRD BASE: The seat at the far left of the table, which is the last to play before the dealer plays his/her hand.

TIE: The result when the player and the dealer finish their hands with the same totals. Also called a push. In blackjack, a tie will often feel like a win.

TRUE COUNT: The running count divided by the number of decks remaining to be seen.

TWENTY–ONE: Another name for the game blackjack; or, the number you are trying to reach with your hand.

UP CARD: The dealer's card that is left face up for the players to see, as opposed to the face-down hole card. All basic strategy is designed based on the dealer's up card.

COMPLETE BASIC STRATEGY

Rows are player's cards. Columns are dealer's upcard.

Baseline rule set (double allowed after splitting, re-split up to three times, dealer stands on all 17s). **Surrender Allowed.**

DEALER'S UPCARD

PLAYER'S CARDS

	2	3	4	5	6	7	8	9	10	A
9	H								H	
10				D						
11										

	2	3	4	5	6	7	8	9	10	A
12	H									
13										
14				S			H			
15										
16									X	

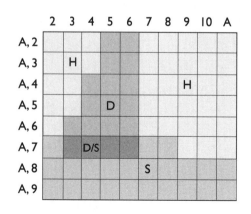

	2	3	4	5	6	7	8	9	10	A
A, 2										
A, 3		H								
A, 4							H			
A, 5				D						
A, 6										
A, 7			D/S							
A, 8						S				
A, 9										

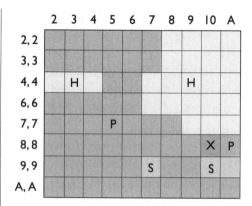

	2	3	4	5	6	7	8	9	10	A
2, 2										
3, 3										
4, 4			H					H		
6, 6										
7, 7				P						
8, 8									X	P
9, 9							S		S	
A, A										

H = Hit
S = Stand
P = Split
D = Double
D/S = Double, or else Stand if you cannot double
X = Surrender

Baseline rule set (double allowed after splitting, re-split up to three times, dealer stands on all 17s). **Surrender *Not* Allowed.**

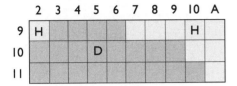

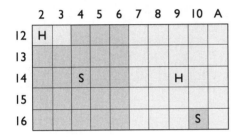

	2	3	4	5	6	7	8	9	10	A
2,2										
3,3										
4,4		H						H		
6,6										
7,7				P						
8,8										
9,9						S			S	
A,A										

H = Hit
S = Stand
P = Split
D = Double
D/S = Double, or else Stand if you cannot double

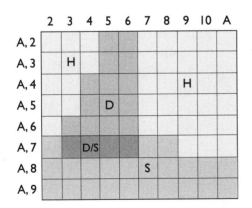

COMPLETE BASIC STRATEGY, DEALER HITS SOFT 17

Rows are player's cards. Columns are dealer's upcard.

Surrender Allowed

DEALER'S UPCARD

PLAYER'S CARDS

	2	3	4	5	6	7	8	9	10	A
9	H								H	
10				D						
11										

	2	3	4	5	6	7	8	9	10	A
12	H									
13										
14				S			H			
15										
16									X	
17										

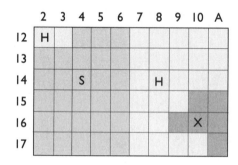

	2	3	4	5	6	7	8	9	10	A
2, 2										
3, 3										
4, 4		H						H		
6, 6										
7, 7			P							
8, 8									X	
9, 9							S		S	
A, A										

H = Hit
S = Stand
P = Split
D = Double
D/S = Double, or else Stand if you cannot double
X = Surrender

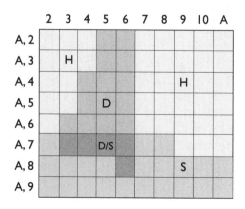

	2	3	4	5	6	7	8	9	10	A
A, 2										
A, 3		H								
A, 4								H		
A, 5				D						
A, 6										
A, 7			D/S							
A, 8								S		
A, 9										

Surrender *Not* Allowed

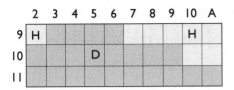

	2	3	4	5	6	7	8	9	10	A
2,2										
3,3										
4,4		H						H		
6,6										
7,7				P						
8,8										
9,9						S			S	
A,A										

	2	3	4	5	6	7	8	9	10	A
9	H								H	
10				D						
11										

	2	3	4	5	6	7	8	9	10	A
12	H									
13										
14			S					H		
15										
16									S	
17										

H = Hit

S = Stand

P = Split

D = Double

D/S = Double, or else Stand if you cannot double

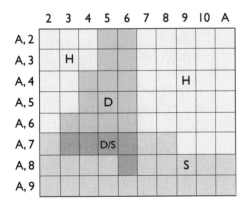

COMPLETE BASIC STRATEGY, NO DOUBLE AFTER SPLITTING

Rows are player's cards. Columns are dealer's upcard.

Surrender Allowed

DEALER'S UPCARD

PLAYER'S CARDS

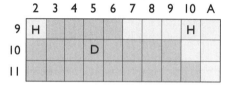

	2	3	4	5	6	7	8	9	10	A
9	H								H	
10				D						
11										

	2	3	4	5	6	7	8	9	10	A
12	H									
13										
14			S				H			
15										
16									X	

	2	3	4	5	6	7	8	9	10	A
2, 2		H			P					
3, 3										
4, 4								H		
6, 6										
7, 7		P								
8, 8									X	P
9, 9							S		S	
A, A										

H = Hit
S = Stand
P = Split
D = Double
D/S = Double, or else Stand if you cannot double
X = Surrender

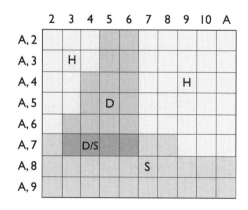

	2	3	4	5	6	7	8	9	10	A
A, 2										
A, 3		H								
A, 4								H		
A, 5				D						
A, 6										
A, 7			D/S							
A, 8						S				
A, 9										

Surrender *Not* Allowed

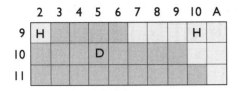

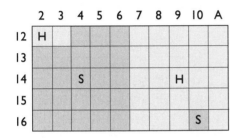

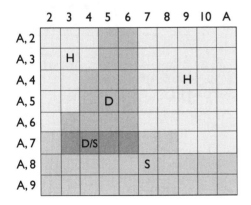

	2	3	4	5	6	7	8	9	10	A
2, 2		H			P					
3, 3										
4, 4								H		
6, 6										
7, 7			P							
8, 8										
9, 9						S			S	
A, A										

H = Hit
S = Stand
P = Split
D = Double
D/S = Double, or else Stand if you
    cannot double

COMPLETE BASIC STRATEGY, NO DOUBLE AFTER SPLITTING, DEALER HITS SOFT 17

Rows are player's cards. Columns are dealer's upcard.

Surrender Allowed

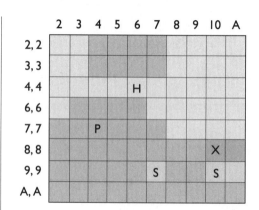

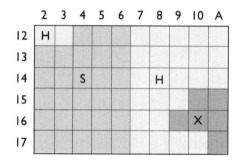

DEALER'S UPCARD

PLAYER'S CARDS

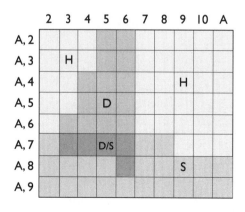

H = Hit
S = Stand
P = Split
D = Double
D/S = Double, or else Stand if you cannot double
X = Surrender

Surrender *Not* Allowed

	2	3	4	5	6	7	8	9	10	A
9	H								H	
10				D						
11										

	2	3	4	5	6	7	8	9	10	A
12	H									
13										
14			S					H		
15										
16									S	
17										

	2	3	4	5	6	7	8	9	10	A
2, 2	H				P					
3, 3										
4, 4								H		
6, 6										
7, 7			P							
8, 8										
9, 9						S			S	
A, A										

H = Hit
S = Stand
P = Split
D = Double
D/S = Double, or else Stand if you
    cannot double

	2	3	4	5	6	7	8	9	10	A
A, 2										
A, 3		H								
A, 4								H		
A, 5				D						
A, 6										
A, 7				D/S						
A, 8								S		
A, 9										

COMPLETE BASIC STRATEGY, ONE DECK

Rows are player's cards. Columns are dealer's upcards.

Baseline rule set (double allowed after splitting, re-split up to three times, dealer stands on all 17s). **Surrender Allowed.**

DEALER'S UPCARD

PLAYER'S CARDS

	2	3	4	5	6	7	8	9	10	A
9	H								H	
10				D						
11										

	2	3	4	5	6	7	8	9	10	A
12	H									
13										
14				S				H		
15										
16									X	

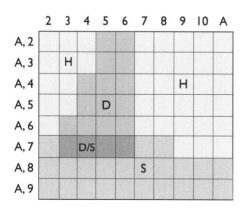

	2	3	4	5	6	7	8	9	10	A
A,2										
A,3			H							
A,4								H		
A,5				D						
A,6										
A,7			D/S							
A,8						S				
A,9										

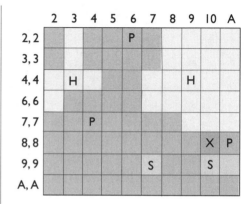

	2	3	4	5	6	7	8	9	10	A
2,2					P					
3,3										
4,4			H					H		
6,6										
7,7			P							
8,8									X	P
9,9								S		S
A,A										

H = Hit
S = Stand
P = Split
D = Double
D/S = Double, or else Stand if you cannot double
X = Surrender

Baseline rule set (double allowed after splitting, re-split up to three times, dealer stands on all 17s). **Surrender Allowed.**

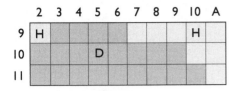

	2	3	4	5	6	7	8	9	10	A
9	H								H	
10				D						
11										

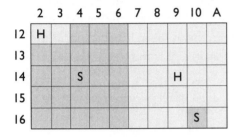

	2	3	4	5	6	7	8	9	10	A
12	H									
13										
14			S					H		
15										
16									S	

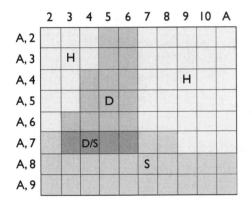

	2	3	4	5	6	7	8	9	10	A
A, 2										
A, 3		H								
A, 4								H		
A, 5				D						
A, 6										
A, 7			D/S							
A, 8						S				
A, 9										

	2	3	4	5	6	7	8	9	10	A
2, 2										
3, 3										
4, 4		H							H	
6, 6										
7, 7				P						
8, 8										
9, 9							S			S
A, A										

H = Hit
S = Stand
P = Split
D = Double
D/S = Double, or else Stand if you cannot double

COMPLETE BASIC STRATEGY, ADJUSTMENT NUMBERS

Rows are player's cards. Columns are dealer's upcard.

Baseline rule set (double allowed after splitting, re-split up to three times, dealer stands on all 17s). **Surrender Allowed. Six- or eight-deck shoes.**

HIT OR STAND

You should stand whenever the true count is equal to or higher than the number in the chart below, and hit when the true count is lower.

DEALER'S UPCARD

PLAYER'S CARDS

	2	3	4	5	6	7	8	9	10	A
12	3	2	0	-1	-3					
13	0	-1	-3	-4	-4					
14	-3	-4	-6					H		
15	-5	-6							4	
16					S			5	0	X
17										-6

WHEN TO DOUBLE

You should double whenever the true count is equal to or higher than the number in the chart below, and hit when the true count is lower.

	2	3	4	5	6	7	8	9	10	A
8			5	3	1			H		
9	1	0	-2	-4	-6	3				
10			D				-6	-4	-1	4	4
11							-6	-4	-4	1

PLAYING ACES

You should double whenever the true count is higher than the number in the chart below. If the true count is not higher than the number, hit or stand according to the corresponding box in that row.

	2	3	4	5	6	7	8	9	10	A
A, 2			3	0	-1					
A, 3	H		1	-1	-4					
A, 4			0	-4		D		H		
A, 5			4	-2	-6					
A, 6	1	-3								
A, 7	0	-2	-6	D/S						
A, 8			5	3	1	1		S		
A, 9				6	5	4				

WHEN TO SPLIT

You should split whenever the true count is higher than the number in the chart below.

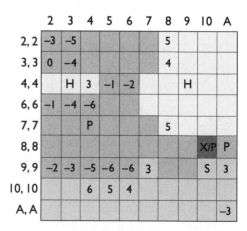

	2	3	4	5	6	7	8	9	10	A
2, 2	-3	-5					5			
3, 3	0	-4					4			
4, 4			H	3	-1	-2		H		
6, 6	-1	-4	-6							
7, 7				P			5			
8, 8									X/P	P
9, 9	-2	-3	-5	-6	-6	3			S	3
10, 10			6	5	4					
A, A										-3

CHAPTER REVIEW ANSWERS

Below are the answers to the review questions at the end of each chapter.

Chapter 1: The Rules of Blackjack

1. 3♥ 5♣ 6♦ 2♣ 4♠
The card values are exactly what you would expect: 3, 5, 6, 2, and 4. The total of the hand is 3+5+6+2+4 = 20.

2. A♦ 8♥
In this hand, the ace takes the value of 11, not 1. The total is 11 + 8 = 19.

3. A♠ 3♠ 8♣ 5♦
In this hand, the ace counts as 1, because if it equaled 11, the hand would bust. The total of the hand is 1+3+8+5 = 17.

4. Player: 3♥ 8♥   Dealer: 6♣
The player has 11 and the dealer shows a 6. The player may hit or stand, as usual. The player may also want to double down. The player cannot split because 3 and 8 are not a pair. Although it would be unorthodox, even stupid, the player could always surrender, as well.

5. Player: 5♠ 5♣   Dealer: J♥
The player has 10 (a pair of 5s) and the dealer shows 10. The player can now do any of the plays: hit, stand, double down, or split the fives. Again, the player could even give up a very good hand and surrender. The dealer may get blackjack with the jack for an up card, but the player can only take insurance if the dealer shows an ace.

6. Player: A♦ 10♣   Dealer: 2♠
In this case, the dealer has a blackjack. Generally, this would be an automatic win at 3:2 odds. However, blackjack rules also say that, if the player wants to take the risk, he can take the hand as 11 rather than 21 and doubl down. (This is not advised, unless the count is very high.)

7. Player: 8♦ 8♦   Dealer: A♠
Again, the player has a pair. He can hit, stand, double down, or split. He can also surrender his 16. Because the dealer is showing an ace, the player can also take insurance before the dealer checks his hole card.

8. A player bets $100 and gets a J♥ A♣. The dealer busts. How much does the player win?
  The player has gotten blackjack. It doesn't even matter that the dealer busts, because as long as the dealer doesn't also get a blackjack, the player will be paid 3:2 odds, or $150.

9. A player bets $100 and gets a 7♥ 7♦. The player splits and gets a 4♣ on the 7♥. He doubles, and gets a Q♠. On his 7♦, he gets a 10♦ and stands. The dealer ends up with 6♦ J♣ 3♥. How much does the player win or lose?

The player splits, betting $100 on each hand. He then doubles the first hand to $200. He ends up with 21 on the first hand and 17 on the second hand. The dealer gets a 19, so the player's first hand wins, but his second hand loses. The player wins $200 for the first hand, but loses $100 on the second, so the total is a $100 win for the player.

10. A player bets $100 and gets A♠ K♠. The dealer is showing A♥. The player takes insurance. The dealer has a 7♣ to go with his A♥. How much does the player win or lose?

If a player gets blackjack and takes insurance, he is guaranteed to win even money, whether the dealer has blackjack or not. In this case, the player would win $150 for the blackjack, but lose $50 on insurance, for a total win of $100 (or even money).

Chapter 3: Basic Blackjack Strategy

1. Player: Q♥ 7♦   Dealer: 3♥
The player has a hard 17. The player should stand.

2. Player: 2♣ 3♣   Dealer: K♥
The player has a hard 5. The player should hit.

3. Player: 9♠ 3♥ 6♠   Dealer: 6♣
The player has a hard 18. The player should stand. (Note that, by basic strategy, this player should not have gotten to this

point. He should have stood with 9♠ 3♥ against the dealer's 6.)

4. Player: 6♦ 5♠   Dealer: J♦
The player has an 11. The player should double against a dealer with 10.

5. Player: 4♥ 5♣   Dealer: 2♠
The player has a 9. The player should hit against a 2. (The player would double if the dealer had any card between 3 and 6.)

6. Player: 2♦ 8♥   Dealer: A♦
The player has a 10. But the dealer is showing an ace, so the player should just hit.

7. Player: 5♠ 5♥   Dealer: 6♣
The player has a pair, so he could split his hand. However, his hand adds up to 10, so he should actually double against the dealer's 6.

8. Player: 7♣ 7♦   Dealer: 4♦
The player has a pair of 7s. The player should split the 7s.

9. Player: 9♥ 9♣   Dealer: 7♠
The player has a pair of 9s. However, the player has a strong hand of 18 against the dealer's 7, so the player should stand.

10. Player: 8♣ 8♠   Dealer: Q♥
The player has a pair of 8s for a total of 16. But the dealer is showing a queen, so the player should surrender. (If surrendering is not allowed, the player would have to split the 8s and hope for some help from the dealer.)

11. Player: A♣ 2♦   Dealer: 4♥
The player has a soft 13. The hand is not strong enough to double, but the player

cannot bust with another card, so the player should hit.

12. Player: A♥ 4♠ 3♣   Dealer: 2♣
The player has a soft 18. If the player had gotten a soft 18 in his first two cards, he would double against the dealer's 2. But, because doubling is not after the third card, the player should stand with 18.

Chapter 4: Rule Variations

(Questions 1-4 assume dealer hits soft 17.)

1. Player: 8♥ 8♦   Dealer: A♠
The player has a pair of 8's for a total of 16. The player should surrender against an ace. (The player would split if the dealer were standing on all 17s.)

2. Player: 8♣ 9♠   Dealer: A♥
The player should surrender with 17 against an ace. (The player would stand if the dealer were standing on all 17s.)

3. Player: Q♦ 5♦   Dealer: A♣
The player has 15. Again, the player should surrender against an ace. (The player would hit if the dealer were standing on all 17s.)

4. Player: 7♣ 4♥   Dealer: A♣
The player has 11. The player should double. (The player would only hit if the dealer were standing on all 17s.)

(Questions 5-8 assume that doubling is not allowed after splitting.)

5. Player: 2♣ 2♦   Dealer: 4♥
This was a trick question. With a pair of 2s against a 4, a player would do the same thing whether doubling after splitting is allowed or not. The player should split. (The player should not split 2s against a 2 or 3, however.)

6. Player: 3♦ 3♠   Dealer: 2♥
The player has a pair of 3s. Just like with a pair of 2s against a 2, the player should only hit when doubling is not allowed after splitting. (The player would split if doubling were allowed.)

7. Player: 6♥ 6♣   Dealer: 2♠
The player should hit the 12 against a 2. (The player would split the 6s if doubling were allowed after splitting.)

8. Player: 4♥ 4♠   Dealer: 6♦
The player should never split a pair of 4s when doubling is not allowed after splitting. The player should just count the hand as 8 and hit.

Chapter 5: Counting Cards

1. A♦ 10♣ 9♦ 2♥ 2♦ 5♠ 6♦ 7♥ 4♣ 4♥ Q♦ 5♥
The values of the cards are:
-1, -1, 0, 1, 1, 1, 1, 0, 1, 1, -1, 1
The running count would be:
-1, -2, -2, -1, 0, 1, 2, 2, 3, 4, 3, 4
The final count is 4.

2. 6♦ 8♠ Q♠ 7♠ 8♦ A♦ K♦ J♥ A♣ 6♠ 6♣ 7♥
The values of the cards are:
1, 0, −1, 0, 0, −1, −1, −1, −1, 1, 1, 0
The running count would be:
1, 1, 0, 0, 0, −1, −2, −3, −4, −3, −2, −2
The final count is −2.

3. 2♦ 5♦ 4♣ 10♦ 7♣ J♣ K♣ 8♣ A♦ 6♣
   J♠ 8♦

The values of the cards are:
1, 1, 1, –1, 0, –1, –1, 0, –1, 1, –1, 0
The running count would be:
1, 2, 3, 2, 2, 1, 0, 0, –1, 0, –1, –1
The final count is –1.

4 . A♦ 4♣ Q♦ Q♣ K♦ 6♥ 5♦ 7♠ 8♥ 7♣
   4♥ 3♠

The values of the cards are:
–1, 1, –1, –1, –1, 1, 1, 0, 0, 0, 1, 1
The running count would be:
–1, 0, –1, –2, –3, –2, –1, –1, –1, –1, 0, 1
The final count is 1.

5. 7♦ 5♣ 9♠ A♣ J♦ 7♣ 7♠ 10♣ 3♦ 2♥
   5♦ Q♣

The values of the cards are:
0, 1, 0, –1, –1, 0, 0, –1, 1, 1, 1, –1
The running count would be:
0, 1, 1, 0, –1, –1, –1, –2, –1, 0, 1, 0
The final count is 0.

6. The relative count is 12. There are three decks remaining in the shoe.

To calculate the true count, divide the relative count by the number of decks remaining. 12 ÷ 3 = 4. The true count is 4.

7. The relative count is 10. You are playing in an eight-deck blackjack game and four decks have been dealt.

Since four decks have been dealt and there are eight decks total, there must be four decks remaining, as well. Divide the relative count (10) by the decks remaining (4). The true count is 2½.

8. The relative count is 12. You didn't sit down until half a deck had already been dealt and there are now only 2 decks left in the shoe. Because you missed half a deck before you sat down, you must add that ½ to the number of decks left before you divide. Therefore, you should divide 12 by 2½. The true count is 5.

Chapter 6: Betting to Win

1. The true count is 5. Your unit bet is $20. The table is using the benchmark rule set.

First, subtract the casino advantage factor from the true count. With the benchmark rule set, the casino advantage factor is ½. Then multiply that number (4½) by your unit bet ($20) to get your optimal bet: $90.

2. The true count is 9. Your unit bet is $100. The rules are the benchmark rules, but doubling is not allowed after splitting. With no doubling after splitting, the casino advantage factor is 1 (½ + ½). Your bet should be (9 – 1) × $100 = $800.

3. The true count is 2. Your unit bet is $50. The rules are the benchmark rules, but early surrender is available.

With early surrender, you subtract 1 from the standard casino advantage factor, to get –½. Then subtract that from the true count, which is the same as adding ½ to the true count (2), to get 2½. Multiply that by your unit bet to get an optimal bet of $125.

4. The true count is –1. Your unit bet is $100. The rules are the benchmark rules.

This is another trick question. If the true count is –1, always bet the minimum allowed (or get up from the table). After all, you can't bet negative $150.

5. The true count is 11. Your unit bet is $10. The rules are the benchmark rules, plus surrender is not available, dealers hit soft 17, and doubling is not allowed after splitting.

The casino advantage factor is ½ + ½ + ½ + ½ = 2. The optimal bet is (11 − 2) × $10 = $90.

Chapter 7: Refining Basic Strategy

1. Player: J♥ 3♦ 3♠   Dealer: K♣
   True Count: −2

The player has 16 against a 10 for the dealer. If the true count were 0 or higher (or unknown) the player would stand, but with a true count of −2, the player should hit.

2. Player: 4♣ 5♣   Dealer: 2♠
   True Count: 3

With a true count of 1 or higher, the player should double (not hit) with 9 against a 2.

3. Player: 8♦ 3♠   Dealer: A♥
   True Count: 1½

When the true count reaches 1, the player should always double with 11, no matter what the dealer's up card is.

4. Player: 5♠ 7♥   Dealer: 3♦
   True Count: 3

With a true count of 2 or higher, the player should stand (not hit) with 12 against a 3.

5. Player: 10♦ 4♥ A♠   Dealer: Q♠
   True Count: 4

The player should stand (not hit) with 15 against 10, when the true count hits 4.

6. Player: 6♣ 4♠   Dealer: A♦
   True Count: 6

The player should always double with 10 when the true count gets to 4 or higher.

7. Player: 3♥ 9♠   Dealer: 4♠
   True Count: −1

With a true count less than zero, the player should hit (not stand) with 12 against a 4.

8. Player: J♣ 6♠   Dealer: J♥
   True Count: −2½

With a true count less than −2, the player should hit 16 against 10, rather than surrendering. Note that at a true count of −2, the player should surrender, but at anything lower (such as −2½), the player should hit.

DO YOU HAVE A PROBLEM?

Gamblers Anonymous offers the following questions to anyone who may have a gambling problem. The questions are provided to help the individual decide if he or she is a compulsive gambler and wants to stop gambling. Most compulsive gamblers will answer yes to at least seven of these questions.

If you need help, you can contact them at:

Gamblers Anonymous
International Service Office
P.O. Box 17173
Los Angeles, CA 90017
(213) 386-8789
www.gamblersanonymous.org

THE TWENTY QUESTIONS

1. Did you ever lose time from work or school due to gambling?
2. Has gambling ever made your home life unhappy?
3. Did gambling affect your reputation?
4. Have you ever felt remorse after gambling?
5. Did you ever gamble to get money with which to pay debts or otherwise solve financial difficulties?
6. Did gambling cause a decrease in your ambition or efficiency?
7. After losing, did you feel you must return as soon as possible and win back your losses?
8. After a win, did you have a strong urge to return and win more?
9. Did you often gamble until your last dollar was gone?
10. Did you ever borrow to finance your gambling?
11. Have you ever sold anything to finance gambling?
12. Were you reluctant to use "gambling money" for normal expenditures?
13. Did gambling make your careless of the welfare of yourself or your family?
14. Did you ever gamble longer than you had planned?
15. Have you ever gambled to escape worry or trouble?
16. Have you ever committed, or considered committing, an illegal act to finance gambling?
17. Did gambling cause you to have difficulty in sleeping?
18. Do arguments, disappointments, or frustrations create within you an urge to gamble?
19. Did you ever have an urge to celebrate any good fortune by a few hours of gambling?
20. Have you ever considered self-destruction or suicide as a result of your gambling?

WHAT IS MENSA? ⓜ

Mensa
The High IQ Society

Mensa is the international society for people with a high IQ. We have more than 100,000 members in over 40 countries worldwide.

The society's aims are:
- to identify and foster human intelligence for the benefit of humanity.
- to encourage research in the nature, characteristics, and uses of intelligence.
- to provide a stimulating intellectual and social environment for its members.

Anyone with an IQ score in the top two percent of population is eligible to become a member of Mensa—are you the "one in 50" we've been looking for?

Mensa membership offers an excellent range of benefits:
- Networking and social activities nationally and around the world
- Special Interest Groups (hundreds of chances to pursue your hobbies and interests—from art to zoology!)
- Monthly International Journal, national magazines, and regional newsletters
- Local meetings—from game challenges to food and drink
- National and international weekend gatherings and conferences
- Intellectually stimulating lectures and seminars
- Access to the worldwide SIGHT network for travelers and hosts

For more information about Mensa International:
www.mensa.org
Mensa International
15 The Ivories
6-8 Northampton Street
Islington, London N1 2HY
United Kingdom

For more information about American Mensa:
www.us.mensa.org
Telephone: 1-800-66-MENSA
American Mensa Ltd.
1229 Corporate Drive West
Arlington, TX 76006 USA

For more information about British Mensa (UK and Ireland):
www.mensa.org.uk
Telephone: +44 (0) 1902 772771
E-mail: enquiries@mensa.org.uk
British Mensa Ltd.
St. John's House
St. John's Square
Wolverhampton WV2 4AH
United Kingdom

For more information about Australian Mensa:
www.au.mensa.org
Telephone: +61 1902 260 594
E-mail: info@au.mensa.org
Australian Mensa Inc.
PO Box 212
Darlington WA 6070 Australia

INDEX

INDEX